Cash for Creatives:

Found Money, Fast Money, Free Money

Part of the MORE MONEY Series

Lindy Schneider

and

Tom L. Schneider

Peaks Publishing Inc
www.PeaksPublishing.com

Schneider, Lindy and Schneider, Tom L.
Cash for Creatives

1. Art 2. Business of art 3. Personal Finance

Summary: How to find money to fund your creative pursuits

ISBN: 978-0-9840385-2-7

Bulk purchases of this book are available at special discounts when purchased for premiums and sales promotions, fundraising or educational use. Special editions or book excerpts can also be created to specifications. Contact Special Sales for Peaks Publishing Inc at www.PeaksPublishing.com.

Cover Illustration by Lindy Schneider
Cover Design by Tom L. Schneider
Title Typeface: Gentium Basic
from www.larabiefonts.com

Printed in the United States of America
Published by Peaks Publishing Inc

Dedication

Creativity is essential to life. From inventions that make our lives easier or that change the world to a simple children's book to change a child, creative artists bring life to our living. Whether adding a voice to an opinion or simply trying to add some beauty in a new way to the world, creative people add richness to our lives.

This book is dedicated to all of those who desire to make their voice heard but have struggled to find the financial resources to bring their creative dreams to reality.

Special thanks go to our four "original creations," our children, whose creative gifts have brought us joy and who have made the world better by sharing their talents.

Other books by Tom L. Schneider and Lindy Schneider:

MORE MONEY in Tough Times: Discover the $10,000 You Never Knew You Had
Part of the MORE MONEY series

Starfish on the Beach
An Amazon best-selling children's book

Table of Contents

Introduction

Every aspiring writer, artist, actor, film maker, musician, and photographer has that moment when he or she is confronted with the question, "Do I give up my dreams and just make a living or do I plow ahead with my creative pursuits and hope I make it big before I starve?"

In the tough economic environment that we are faced with today that question becomes even more difficult to answer. It is as though the world is spinning so fast and generating so many bills that the ability to stop just long enough to create something for the sheer joy of self expression is almost impossible.

Some artists have creative ideas that they believe they could build into a profitable business but they need a helping hand to get started. Unfortunately, these artists find that banks will not loan money for most creative ventures and the philanthropic giants that could help an artist get a creative business started are nowhere to be found.

If this describes some of your frustrations you have come to the right book. Do not give up your dreams! We are on a mission to show creative individuals how they can survive in this economy and still pursue their passion.

That's why we created the *Cash for Creatives System*. It is a financial roadmap for creative individuals like yourself to follow that will guide you on your way to achieving your creative goals, whether full or part time.

The *Cash for Creatives System* opens three powerful sources of money to you if you are willing to put in the effort to follow the instructions. These sources are grouped under chapters entitled *Found Money, Fast Money* and *Free Money*.

Unlike applying for grants, loans or government assistance, all three of these sources are under your control! They are not dependent upon a small jury's subjective judgment. They are also not dependent on your finding a few large patrons who will support your creative goals.

Instead, simply by following the steps in the *Cash for Creatives System* outlined in this book you may be able to bring your creative projects to life in ways you never thought possible. Each of the steps will bring you closer to reaching your financial goals and bringing you the money you need to let the world see your creative side.

Start at the Beginning - Always a Good Place to Start

The beauty of these three money sources is that any one of them can be effective on its own. We strongly recommend you read through this book beginning with Found Money in chapter one doing all the things that we recommend, then move on to Chapter Two and so on.

Now you might be tempted to skip right to the chapter on Free Money, but we recommend you don't. If you do you will be missing out on some powerful money generating ideas that can speed your creative dreams along.

In order to achieve the maximum potential of funding your creative project you'll need to utilize all of the components in this book, so approach this process methodically. When you work all of these three powerful sources together, just like a three-legged easel, you will have a much more secure base on which to build your artistic endeavors.

Make these changes a habit and you can permanently change your life for the better. It will also help ensure that you will have the money you will need for future projects as well.

Also, one final note before we begin. We use the term "artist" throughout this book to represent all of the creative arts. Our use of this word is intentional, because if you are a creative you are an artist, whether a musician, a writer, an actor, an inventor, a film maker, a photographer, a sculptor, or - yes - even a painter. Artists simply choose different mediums to present their creative work. The concepts and steps in this book can work for any creative person who chooses to pursue their dreams. Hopefully one of them is you!

"Your circumstances do not determine your future. Your responses to those circumstances do."

- Lindy Schneider

1 The Three Money Sources

My parents were both artists, so I (Lindy) was raised in an art rich environment. Instead of family picnics we had family sketch outings to the park where it was more important to bring our sketch books and pencils than the picnic lunch. As a family we traveled to see art shows and art museums.

One summer my parents took my sisters and me on a trip to see the biggest stone sculptures I had ever seen. The likenesses of George Washington, Thomas Jefferson, Teddy Roosevelt, and Abe Lincoln were carved right into Mount Rushmore! It captivated my mind. This art project took 14 years and one million dollars with 100 people working full time to bring it to completion.

On that same road trip we drove to see an even bigger sculpture in progress. The artist, Korczak Ziolkowski, was carving the likeness of Chief Crazy Horse into a mountain. His dream was to carve the entire mountain to resemble Chief Crazy Horse mounted upon his steed.

I remember squinting at the mountain to try to make out the rough form of the Indian chief that the artist had been working on for years. To me it still just looked like a mountain. In the visitors center there were donation buckets all around the room appealing to the tourists to help keep the project going. If there were no funds the artist's work would have to stop.

Decades later my husband Tom and I returned to the sight of the Chief Crazy Horse monument and although the face was now visible I again found myself squinting to try to identify the image of the great warrior on his horse. Instead of being a monument to a great warrior it seemed more like a monument to an artist's lack of funds.

Now, it can be argued that Ziolkowski's dream was too ambitious for any one man, or even his family. He began the work in 1920 and died in 1982, but his wife and seven of his ten children have carried on the project.

What is inarguable is that an artist needs more than talent, more than training and more than a creative vision. An artist needs money for materials and living expenses to be able to pursue his or her passion, and sometimes he or she needs help from others. Unfortunately, very few artists are chosen to receive grants and banks laugh at loaning money for most creative pursuits.

So, how do you find the money to see your dream project through to completion? In this book you will discover where to find money enough to create your dream project. You will also discover where you can get help from others. We will walk you through the very same steps that Tom and I took to fund our dream project, but you will be able to do it in a lot less time. That's because we've already dug up the resources and walked the steps ourselves.

Our Creative Project

We started our own journey with a dream and some substantial skills we had acquired over the years. Tom is an accomplished writer having worked as both a technical and feature writer for numerous companies and publications. He has also won national awards for his songwriting, marketing and sales.

I have created illustrations for magazines and publishing houses for several years. I also am a contributing author for several of the New York Times #1 Best Selling *Chicken Soup for the Soul* series books and an award winning playwright.

We've been self employed most of our adult lives. In our jobs we've needed to continually seek out new clients in order to make a living. We often worked long days and sometimes on the weekends as well. We also had parenting, church and community responsibilities we had chosen to take on. That didn't leave us a lot of time for our creative pursuits.

While being self employed was always rewarding (though not always monetarily) our dream was to write, illustrate and publish a children's book and print it in large enough quantities that we could give copies to a charity that provides books to children being rescued from abusive situations.

In what limited spare time I had I would work on the watercolor illustrations for the book, then tuck them back into my portfolio waiting for the day when we had saved up enough money to have the project printed. We wanted to bring this dream to reality, but we became discouraged at how long it was taking to raise the money needed. It seemed there was always something unexpected that arose that demanded our savings as well as our time.

Still the passion was in our hearts. We began to research and interview other professionals as to how they were able to raise the money for their dream projects. Slowly, like archaeologists unearthing rare treasures we discovered sources of money that we could use to finally fund our dream.

This new found knowledge gave us the ability to finally see our dream become a reality. Our children's book, *Starfish on the Beach* (available at Amazon.com) reached its funding goal and has since become an Amazon best seller.

You are an artist and you, too, have dreams. You have hopes and creative passion or you would not have been attracted to this book. This book will not give you talent or art training. It will not give you courage to show your work to the world. However, if money is all that is holding you back, you have come to the right place for help. When you have the money that you need to pursue your dream, you will be amazed at your courage to forge ahead and be the artist you hoped you could be.

In the following pages we are going to reveal to you some of the money secrets that Tom and I discovered. So, dust off your dreams and renew your hopes. If you need money for art supplies, you can have it. If you need living expenses to free your time to write that book you've had inside you for years, we will show you how you can find that time. That music CD or film that tells your story is finally within your reach. If your dream is to travel to Italy and paint landscapes to have a solo show you will discover how even that is possible through our *Cash for Creatives System.*

Now, raising the amount of funds it would take to complete the lifelong venture that the Chief Crazy Horse Monument demands is raising the stakes too high for a starting point, but choosing a project within a $1,000 to $20,000 range is very doable. If you think that amount of money would help you get started then let Tom and I, America's Money Archaeologists, lead you to the sites that contain money you didn't know was there.

The Cash for Creatives System

As with any journey there are certain steps you need to take to prepare for a successful trip. On this adventure we will need to work on three separate but necessary components. Think of it as a three-legged easel holding up your dream picture.

The first leg is **Found Money.** This is the first aid you need to administer to your finances so that the following two phases will not be sabotaged by "blood loss." We will show you how you can reallocate the money that you are now earning and spending for survival to make it stretch further, leaving you extra money to pursue your dreams.

The second leg to securing the money you need for your dream project is **Fast Money.** In this chapter you will discover how to use what you already know or have on hand to generate cash right away. There are things that you can teach or services you can provide right now to generate extra money quickly.

We will walk you through several ideas to get you moving toward your goal. By putting one or more of these ideas in place immediately you will generate the momentum you need to propel you forward into the third phase.

The third leg of the easel we call **Free Money.** In this chapter we will show you in detail how to use a crowdfunding site to inspire others to give (not loan) you large sums of money specifically for your project. You will also be generating loyal patrons at the same time.

Thousands of artists have failed to achieve their dreams because they didn't have the knowledge or expertise to market their careers effectively. In many cases it was simply because they couldn't generate the initial money needed to get their dreams moving forward.

This is why we developed the *Cash for Creatives System. The Cash for Creatives System* can kick start or restart any artist's career. Now it is time to kick start yours!

"When you fully understand how many hours of your life it takes to earn $100 you'll think twice about how easily you spend it. You can't buy any more time at any price, so spend wisely."

- Tom Schneider

2 Found Money: Discover the Hundreds of Dollars You Didn't Know You Had

(The following ideas are excerpted from MORE MONEY in Tough Times: Discover the $10,000 You Never Knew You Had *published by Peaks Publishing Inc. Available from Amazon.com or PeaksPublishing.com)*

If it seems your money doesn't stretch as far these days, you're not alone. An Associated Press article dated September 2011 reported that there are now a record 46.2 million people in this country who can be classified as poor — nearly 1 in 6 Americans. The prolonged recession has left millions struggling and out of work.

Do you relate to that news? It is hard enough to keep the lights on and food in the refrigerator, but as an artist you have paints, brushes and canvases to buy just to continue to exercise your talents. Coming up with enough extra money to finance a solo art show is out of the question.

As a film maker your expenses to produce a movie are even higher. There is equipment to rent, actors and crew to hire, locations to rent, craft service, and a host of other expenses.

As a writer you don't have a lot of out of pocket expenses, but the one thing you can't buy at any price is enough *time* to complete your manuscript. You have to spend most of your time just earning a living. You simply have too many bills to pay *right now!*

Everyone seems to be looking for the additional resources to make their lives more comfortable and fulfilling.

Found Money

Very few of us have the luxury of enough time or money to fully pursue our dreams. The good news is that in following through on this first leg of the *Cash for Creatives System* called the **Found Money** process you will discover there are ways to make your current income stretch further than you imagined possible. You will also be learning a way of living that will keep your money from needlessly bleeding away.

It is actually quite simple to find extra money if you know where to look. It is nothing more than identifying where you spend your money and then finding more efficient ways to accomplish the same objective.

With a minimal amount of effort and some basic awareness of your spending habits you can uncover simple ways to save money without the pain of giving up all the things you enjoy most. Does this sound too good to be true? Perhaps this example will help illustrate the point.

The Bathtub

We had a dripping faucet in our bathtub for several months. A drop every few seconds was not a high enough priority for me to take the time to fix it or spend the money on a plumber. After all, it was just a few drips.

One day Lindy was cleaning the tub and inadvertently left the drain plug closed. The faucet continued to drip as before. We were shocked the next day to find the tub filled 6 inches deep with water! That small drip had resulted in gallons of water wasted in just one day. We were literally throwing money down the drain.

We learned two things from this experience. First, we needed to pay more attention to the "small" ways we were wasting money. We had to recognize the long term cost before we were motivated to address the problem. Secondly, we realized how much we would be saving over time by simply "fixing" those small financial drips.

We fixed the faucet and stopped wasting the money we had been spending on water for which we weren't getting any benefit. We then were able to take the money we had been wasting and put it to work for us elsewhere.

To find the extra money you need to fund your creative project you must first "fix" the things that are draining your finances without significant benefit. You can then take the money you save and use it for things that will be of more value to you both today and in the future.

In order to know where you can *save* money you first need to learn where you are *spending* your money. You have to buy food, gas, insurance and pay your utility bills. You also need to keep your heart happy by spending money on entertainment occasionally.

If you could save even $100 per month by changing how you spend your money you could set aside $1,200 in one year. By reallocating a few dollars more here and there you would have a sizable amount to work with.

This is saved money without any increase in pay or reduction in lifestyle! It's like getting a raise in pay without having to rely on your employer. Look at your monthly spending as you would an unfinished sculpture and see what you can chisel away and refine to make your life sculpture that much more valuable.

We've included some simple ideas on the following pages that can start you on your way toward more efficient spending and result in substantial savings to you. Most of these suggestions can be implemented with a minimum of effort but they won't help you if you don't take advantage of them. Use this "found" money as the starting point on your journey toward funding your creative dreams.

A Word About Potential Savings

The following suggestions will show you ways to save more of the money you are already earning. After each of these suggestions is a potential savings listed. These are what a person can reasonably expect to save if they take advantage of that suggestion. Please note that these are not *guaranteed* savings and are included as guidelines only. Your actual savings may be higher or lower than those listed after each suggestion.

How to Save On Food

1) Don't be chicken to try this

Let's say you buy one meal out every day for lunch. You are being thrifty and you buy a chicken sandwich at a deli for $5. It is good and you are full for one meal, but you are out $5.

Now, let's say you reallocate that $5 to buy a rotisserie cooked chicken at the grocery store. Take the chicken home, cut all the meat off and throw the bones away. You will have over three cups of cooked chicken. With that you can make 6 chicken sandwiches, or 6 chicken tortilla wraps. You could make six plates of chicken cheese quesadillas, or a full pot of chicken soup that would feed six!

Try bringing your own lunch to work at least two days a week and you'll be surprised how quickly the savings add up. You may spend an additional $3 for the tortillas, cheese or vegetables for the soup but instead of spending $30 to buy a sandwich out every day for 6 days you spend only $8 to eat for 6 days.

Potential Savings: If you did this just one week a month you could save around $25/month - that's $300 in one year! It's that easy to put hundreds of dollars back in your pocket or make it available to pursue your creative goals.

2) Drink it up

How many sodas do you drink in a week? Even the super-sized cups for $1 can really add up. Just one a day will cost you over $30/month. Over the course of a year you will spend over $350 just on sodas! What's worse is that even the sugar free varieties are loaded with chemicals and other additives that can do long term damage to your health.

Why not try a low cost, healthier substitute? Flavored iced teas are not only just as tasty but have substantial health benefits as well. You can get flavored tea mixes in your local grocery store that will make up to 36 quarts of tea for under $6! Both sugared and sugar free options are available in a variety of flavors, including raspberry, peach, lemon and even mango.

Most varieties also contain 100% of your daily vitamin C requirement. Even people who have never liked tea will like these delicious, healthier alternatives to soda. You can save hundreds of dollars a year with this tasty treat, be healthier and all you'll be missing is the fizz!

Potential Savings: Even compared to the $1 "super-guzzler" sized soft drinks at the local convenience store, one container of iced tea mix can save you over $22/month compared to buying one of those unhealthy soda drinks a day. Over the course of a year this can save an individual $200-$300 if you drink one glass a day instead of buying that soda. Families could save $300-$500 or more. The "hidden" savings of less medical issues by consuming healthier beverages adds even more value to this tip.

Bonus Tip: If coffee is your drink of choice and you just *have* to have your favorite coffee shop's coffee every day, why not buy the beans and brew your cup at home a couple of days a week? You'll save over $2.50/cup and not sacrifice the flavor. This simple change can save you $20/month or over $300/year! As you can see, small changes result in hundreds of dollars in "change" over the course of a year.

3) Mix it up

Let's face it. We are all busy and sometimes we just don't have time to make a meal from scratch. Eating out can be a real budget-buster if you do it too frequently. To make meal time at home easier and less time consuming, make your own convenience mixes so they'll be ready when you need them. You'll save both time and money and can include only the ingredients you like.

Taco seasoning, spaghetti seasoning, brownie mix, cookie mix, muffins, pancakes, biscuits - the list of possible mixes goes on. You can make your own mixes or sauces for a fraction of what you would pay for them in the store and have them available whenever you need a quick mix.

To make a dry mix that you can store on your shelf for months you can go to:

allrecipes.com

Search for "Taco Seasoning Mix" or "Biscuit Mix", for example. Note how many servings the recipe says it will make. The site includes a handy portion guide calculator function that lets you choose how many servings you want to prepare and it automatically reconfigures the ingredient measurements for you. In most cases it will let you measure out enough for as low as two servings.

Start with two servings. Measure out all the dry ingredients and mix them together. Pour the mixed dry ingredients into a tablespoon or measuring cup to see how much it measures. Write this down; it is the amount of the combined dry mix you will need to make the two serving recipe when you are actually cooking the meal.

Now use the portion guide calculator again to make several more servings of the dry mix and store it in a jar with a tightly fitting lid.

Create a label for this jar with the amount of each dry ingredient to make the bulk mix for when you run out. Also, create a label with the full instructions for making the recipe for the two serving meal.

So how does this save you money? First, you won't be buying those pre-packaged seasonings for tacos or those jars of spaghetti sauce. Add your own self-made taco seasonings to ground beef and you saved over $1. Add tomato sauce and your personal seasoning mix to create your own delicious spaghetti sauce or pizza sauce for less than half the cost of buying a jar of pre-made sauce.

By preparing these mixes in advance you can cook up a meal just as fast as if you were opening a seasoning package or jar and doing it for less money. The mixes are easy to store and you never need to worry about running out. You'll also save the time and expense of running to the grocery store for that jar of spaghetti sauce or spending that $10-$20 for hamburgers or pizza for the family.

Potential Savings: Individuals can easily save $50 - $100/year by using their own mixes. Families could see savings of $150 - $250. Having these mixes available will also save you several "meals out" to save you hundreds of dollars more. The added benefit of eliminating a few extra trips to the store to get the seasoning jar or package you ran out of can save you additional time and money as well.

4) Stock it Up

Get into the habit of stocking up on foods you eat on a regular basis. Make a master list of foods you eat often: chicken, hamburger, breakfast cereals, bread, butter, tomato sauce, etc. Virtually anything that can be frozen or stored on a pantry shelf for a time is a potential "stock-up" item. When one of the things on your main list goes on sale buy enough at the reduced price to get you through 1-3 months for each item.

Meats and frozen goods generally go on sale every 4-6 weeks, so you won't need to stock up on as much at one time. Canned goods and cereals generally have a 3 month cycle between sales, so better to plan for a 3 month supply when stocking up on these items.

If you live in a metro area where there are several grocery stores within a few miles you can maximize your savings further and stock up less.

Each store has a different cycle of specials and "loss leaders" (items put on sale at or below their cost to entice you to shop there). One store may have chicken breasts on sale one week, and another store may follow suit a week or two later. By shopping the specials on a grocery store "route" and buying the specials at each store during the week you can often save nearly as much as you are spending. Cutting your food budget by 40% or more is worth a few extra stops at multiple stores.

TIP: Talk to your local grocery store manager. They can often tell you the schedule of when certain items are going to be back on sale so you can plan accordingly.

Potential Savings: Because your food budget is such a substantial percentage of your overall monthly budget your savings can be very substantial as well. Expect annual savings of at least $400 for an individual and up to $2,000 or more for families with children compared to buying those same items at regular retail price.

5) How do things measure up?

Coupons can be a great way to save money on groceries, but coupons often require you to buy multiples of the same items in order to get the savings. Grocery stores are also increasingly offering deals when you purchase 10 or more items that are part of the promotion. They don't have to be the same item, but are always part of a select collection of items.

Here is where smart shoppers can maximize their savings. For multiple items of the same kind compare the cost/unit of the larger package vs. buying multiples of the smaller packages. If the coupon discount results in greater savings by purchasing the smaller size package than buying the larger package buy two or three of the smallest package size. Two 12 oz. boxes of cereal that allow you to save $1 might be a better deal than buying two 24 oz. packages.

To determine the best value compare the unit price *after* the coupon savings. The cost/ounce or other measurement is the best way to compare prices. Simply divide the package size by the number of ounces to determine the cost/ounce. Buy the package size that gives you the lowest per unit price. You'll often find it is better to buy multiples of the smaller packages than the larger ones.

If you are not using coupons but instead are just taking advantage of the "buy 10 and save $5" type deals it is almost always a better deal to buy multiples of the smaller sizes. The money back is based on the number of items, not the price or size of each item, so unless there is a dramatic difference in unit cost among sizes, go for the smaller size and make sure you get the number of items you need to get the special deal.

Additional Tip: With those "buy 10 save $5" promotions, consider buying 10 of the least expensive items that qualify for the savings. Remember, it is *any* 10 items. Don't buy larger items just to make your quota of 10 when you can buy 10 less expensive items that you would normally buy anyway.

Also, don't buy 10 items if you only need three! Better to pay a higher price for three items you actually need than to buy 10 items that you wouldn't normally want or use just to take advantage of the "savings".

Potential Savings: Savings can average 15 - 30% or more with these deals. If you can save just $5-$10/week you could see an annual savings of $250 for individuals, $500 or more for families.

How to Save On Utilities

There are many ways to cut expenses and still live better. While your grocery bill may be one of your major budget items, you can still save in a variety of other ways as well. Energy conservation is an easy yet painless way to save money. Some simple advance planning and a little "habit modification" will result in significant savings throughout the year. So turn up the heat on energy savings and keep your energy expenses from giving you the cold shoulder.

6) Turn down the water and wrap up in a blanket

Your water heater is one of the prime energy users in your house. By turning down the thermostat on your water heater you can save a bundle each year in energy bills, so turn down the heat. You'll still have plenty of hot water and won't run as great a risk of being scalded by tap water that is too hot.

If your water heater is located in your garage like many of them are these days, you might also want to consider getting a water heater blanket. They are simply insulated "cloaks" that wrap around your water heater to keep the hot in and the cold air out. Most home supply stores carry them. Just be sure to follow the instructions that come with the blanket. This simple and inexpensive device can be installed in a manner of minutes.

You can still experience savings if you purchase a water heater blanket for your indoor water heater. While the savings will be less substantial, the extra insulation will make your heater run less and still save you money year round.

Potential Savings: Turning the temperature down on your water heater by 10 degrees can save you over $60/year. By adding a water heater blanket you can save an additional $30-$100/year in energy costs, depending on your local climate and where in your home your water heater is located. The US Dept of Energy estimates savings of between 25 and 45% in energy savings by using a water heater blanket.

7) Laundering Money

This again is one of those “small” changes you can make that over the course of the year can result in some measurable savings. When doing your laundry, always set the rinse cycle on your washing machine to cold water. The temperature of your rinse water will not affect how clean your clothes get or how well detergent is removed from your clothes, but will save you money in electric or gas bills.

Likewise, a little preventive maintenance on your dryer can save you energy as well. First, make sure the lint trap is cleaned after every dryer load. Also, make sure the exhaust tube that extends from the back of your dryer to the outside remains clear of lint. Even a modest obstruction can make your clothes take longer to dry and result in wasted energy.

Potential Savings: By using the cold water cycle for your rinse you can save over 1000 gallons of hot water a year as an individual, or up to 5,000 gallons a year for an active family. That's thousands of gallons of water that doesn't have to be heated.

Depending on the efficiency of your water heater savings can range from $30/year for an individual to well over $150/year for a family. You'll also save on your water bills if you have a municipal water source. Cleaning your lint trap and keeping the exhaust tube clear can save you an additional $50/year in utility costs.

How to Save On Automobile Expenses

Your car is usually an essential part of your life. Unless you live in an urban area and can always use public transportation you're going to incur some substantial expenses just to get around. Here are some tips to ease the pain of car expenses.

8) Insure your future by shopping around

If you own a car you need to have auto insurance. You can insure your future savings by getting competitive bids on your auto insurance every year or two. Insurance companies change their rate structures from year to year, and often charge lower rates to new customers than they do for existing customers. Companies trying to win a larger share of a local or regional market may offer incentives or preferred rates to motorists with good driving records. Don't pay more for comparable coverage than you have to.

A word of caution, however: make sure you are actually comparing "apples to apples" coverage. Get a quote to compare to your exact existing coverage. Check different companies for any "extras" they include in their rates like free roadside assistance, extended coverage for rental cars, etc.

Be sure to ask what kinds of discounts you might qualify for such as safe driver discounts, anti-lock brake discounts, etc. Some companies can save you up to 40% by taking advantage of all the varying discounts.

Finally, ask for an itemized breakdown of the quoted rate. Some of the above "free extras" may *not* be free at all, but the agent makes extra commission by adding them into your quote. If you have AAA, for example, you won't get any extra benefit by that roadside assistance "extra" from your car insurance. If it reduces your premiums, take it out.

Shopping for any kind of insurance is not usually someone's favorite way to spend their time, but taking the time necessary to actually compare specifics of coverage can save you hundreds of dollars if you have a major claim at some point in the future.

Potential Savings: Don't always believe those "15 minutes can save you 15% on your car insurance" commercials. Check it out yourself and get several estimates from half a dozen companies, then choose the best fit and savings. The few hours you will need to get the best deal will be paying you handsomely in the money you will save. Depending on the number of cars you own and how comprehensive your coverage is you can easily save $400-$500/year simply by spending a few hours shopping wisely.

9) Go the extra mile(s)

We all know we should change the oil in our car at regular intervals, but you may be spending more on oil changes than necessary. Your service station may want you to change your oil every 3,000 miles, but today's cars can almost always go 5,000, even 7,500 miles or more before requiring an oil change.

A majority of cars on the road today have an oil index sensor that tells you when you *really* need to change your oil. Trust the gauge and not your oil change dealer. If you don't have an indicator, check your user's manual for the correct interval for oil changes, then save the money and the time by stopping in for oil changes less frequently.

Potential Savings: If you travel just 15,000 miles a year you would need 5 oil changes if you followed your service station's advice. You can save two oil changes a year by following the auto manufacturer's recommendations and your index sensor without risking any damage to your engine. You'll save $70 or more/year, hours of time, and help to conserve our oil resources. Pretty slick!

How to Save On Entertainment

Let's face it: we all need a little "fun" time to keep our creative edge. The key is to find ways to afford the fun you need while still saving money.

As a creative person it is important that you get out of your studio or office regularly and experience new things. It helps to keep your right brain happy and a happy right brain is a creative right brain.

The following tips will give you a chance to enjoy life a little more while still spending your money efficiently.

10) Fun at half the price (or even less!)

If you like to do special things but don't have the cash for a riverboat ride or horseback riding in the mountains check out either of these websites:

LivingSocial.com
Groupon.com

They offer huge daily discounts on special events. Discounts range from 40% to as high as 90%. They will send you daily emails about the deal of the day in your area. Just sign up and get deals like we did. We signed up through LivingSocial.com and got a $130/person horseback riding trip in the mountains for $49 each.

They have smaller deals as well like the time we bought a $20 gift card for Cinnabons (a great cinnamon roll shop) for only $10. It was a great ease-the-stress cheap date to go buy amazing cinnamon rolls and coffee. You can even access the daily deal for other cities in the United States in case you are planning a trip or want to get a gift for someone who lives in another part of the country.

Living Social even offers incentives for you to get the daily deal *free*. Once you have signed up, simply send the link about the daily deal to your friends. If three of them sign up to join you, your purchase will be free! Now that's a deal you can live with and you get rewarded just for sharing it with your friends. Anyone up for a rafting trip?

Potential Savings: If you take advantage of just one of the daily deals every two months your savings can be from $100-$500 or more a year. For couples and families look for savings of between $200 and $800, and you'll have some great memories of your adventures to share with each other and photos to paint from for years to come.

11) Freebies for your birthday

As children we enjoyed having a birthday party with cake, ice cream, and pizza. As adults we don't seem as eager to celebrate our increasing years and most of us feel uncomfortable about throwing a party for ourselves.

Now there is a way to celebrate your birthday guilt-free. Go to:

FreeBirthdayTreats.com

This website lists a wide variety of restaurants, entertainment venues and other businesses that offer special deals to you on your birthday or during your birthday month. Simply scroll through the offers and sign up for the e-clubs you are interested in. Some special offers do not even require you to sign up in advance. Simply show your ID on your birthday and get the birthday deal.

While not exclusively food related, this site specializes in food outlets where you can get a variety of free meals, free desserts or other free or steeply discounted offers for your birthday. Some e-clubs even send you an extra offer just for signing up. You'll get occasional emails from them year round about special offers given only to e-club members. These "member only" deals are a great way to eat out for less and celebrate your birthday in guilt-free style!

The birthday freebies and discounts aren't limited to meals, however. You can get free oil changes, movie tickets, bowling, even ski for free at certain ski resorts. Some retail stores offer special discounts on your birthday.

It has been said that with age comes wisdom. Be wise enough to take advantage of some of these special deals to help you celebrate getting older and bring back a little of that childhood excitement about your birthday.

Plan on having a month of entertainment since many of these deals can be used anytime during the month or within two weeks of your birthday.

Tip: Sign up for the e-clubs at least a month in advance of your birthday so that they have you in the system in time for your big day. Plan your month to take maximum advantage of the special birthday offers. Schedule which deals to enjoy each day in advance to maximize your gifts and savings. It definitely makes getting older something to look forward to.

Potential Savings: Many of these free meals can save you $7-$18. If you take advantage of several of them during your birthday season you can save $40-$75 in just meals. Add in the entertainment savings and you can save an additional $20-$50. For couples or families these savings can be expanded greatly and can result in savings of up to $300 or more per year.

How to Save Thousands More

The ideas we have listed here are just to get you started. While we can't guarantee how much money you will save, if you follow through on all of them you could save as much as $2,500 in one year. That is money you can then apply to getting your creative project moving forward. By applying these savings to what you will learn in the following chapters you will have a strong foundation upon which to build your creative career.

The savings ideas in this chapter have been excerpted from our book *MORE MONEY in Tough Times: Discover the $10,000 You Never knew You Had* published by Peaks Publishing Inc.

MORE MONEY in Tough Times will show you over 100 ways to spend your money more efficiently without budgeting, cutting up your credit cards or reducing your lifestyle. It is available on Amazon.com or directly from the publisher at:

PeaksPublishing.com

"Just don't give up trying to do what you really want to do. Where there is love and inspiration, I don't think you can go wrong."

-Ella Fitzgerald

3 Fast Money - What You Can Do Right Now to Generate Extra Cash

When money is hard to come by people tighten their belts and figure out ways to spend less. In the previous chapter we showed you ways you can keep more of your money without negatively impacting your lifestyle. In this chapter you will move to the second phase of the Cash for Creatives System and discover how you can quickly get more money coming in to your bank account.

When you are in need of some extra cash having something you can offer to sell that doesn't cost you lots of time or expensive supplies to create is ideal. The challenge is in finding something you are willing to part with that is of sufficient value. It also has to be something you can sell relatively easily and quickly. But what if you don't have a lot of things of value that you can you sell quickly?

It used to be that real estate was what people wanted to buy above all else. If you had property to sell you could turn it into cash within a month or two. When the bottom dropped out of the housing market, however, people shied away from investing in houses.

Paintings, sculptures, collectibles and antiques were other things that people with money snatched up. Again, the economic uncertainties of today have made many people pull back from investing in those items as well.

The one thing that *is* selling like crazy is information. People want to know more about any number of things and are willing to pay for that training and expertise.

So stop and ask yourself; what do I know right now that I can teach to others to generate more money? Do you have education (formal or apprenticeship training) in a particular area that you could share? Have you discovered a way of making contacts in your industry that others would love to learn?

As an artist you have talents and abilities that people admire and are willing to pay you to learn. You may have some insights into how to address certain problems common to organizations or businesses that you could share for a fee.

James Malinchak, the highly successful and highly paid speaker, author and coach who was featured on ABCs *The Secret Millionaire* told Tom and I that the fastest way to wealth is to do something, teach it, write about it and sell it.

The key here is to break down what you know into smaller chunks of information. Instead of a class on "How to Survive as a Professional Artist" offer several smaller classes: "How to Prepare for An Art Show" or "How to Audition for a Commercial." These are important aspects of the creative industry that others just starting out would love to learn.

You may not be far enough along in your knowledge of a particular subject to feel confident about teaching it. Don't let this prevent you from teaching it anyway! As long as you know more about your subject than your attendees you have something valuable to offer.

Teaching something as basic as "How to Prepare for Your First Art Show" can be a valuable course for someone just starting out in the art business, for example. You may have only done two or three shows yourself but your knowledge and expertise is still valuable to those who don't know these basics.

Other businesses can benefit from your knowledge as well. As an artist or photographer, you know how to use color, you know how to create a pleasing composition, you understand symmetry and design that can make ads more appealing. You may even know different computer programs that you use to help you with your art or business and can teach those programs to others.

You may also be able to market those services directly to businesses. Instead of teaching them the software and other information, offer to create their products *for* them and you do the work! You can develop a steady repeat business marketing what you already know.

If you are a film maker you know how to create a suspenseful or anticipatory mood in a film through lighting and music. Teaching this knowledge to a business that needs to create an inexpensive video for personnel training that will hold the interest of the employees, for example, could be very helpful to the business and profitable for you. In many cases they will hire you to do the video for them.

Actors know how to speak in a way that grabs attention and writers know how to write the speaker's script to grab the audience's heart. All these elements are essential to the success of any marketing program. Businesses and individuals are eager to learn what you know and will pay for the opportunity to either have you teach them how to do it themselves or will hire you, as the expert, to do it for them.

Don't be afraid to go outside of your creative niche to find things you can share with a paying audience, either. Be creative about all of the places you might be able to provide information that others would find valuable. You might just come up with a project or idea for someone else they didn't even know they could benefit from until you mentioned it. Always be on the lookout for ways to market yourself and your expertise.

Following are a couple of examples of how others are using their skills to make Fast Money:

Karen Vance - Oil Painter

Karen Vance (www.KarenVanceArt.com) is a nationally recognized fine artist whose oil paintings have won many awards and typically sell for 4 and 5 figures. Her work is part of prominent collections including the permanent collection of The Whitney Gallery of Western Art in Cody, Wyoming hanging alongside C.M. Russell and Albert Bierstadt paintings.

Vance produces about 50 original paintings each year. She expands her income base by producing limited edition giclées (high-end prints) of her work. The price point of a giclée is less than 10% of the price of one of her original paintings, allowing a larger demographic of collectors to own a beautiful image of her work. The giclée reproduction of Vance's original painting then generates several additional sales after the original painting is sold without taking any more of her studio time.

Judging art shows and competitions, giving art demonstrations, presenting lectures and teaching workshops are other things she does periodically to supplement her income and to gain more exposure for her work. She also speaks at events on non-art topics as well.

Susan Blackwood and Howard Friedland - Oil Painters

Susan Blackwood (www.SusanBlackwood.com) and her husband Howard Friedland (www.HowardFriedland.com) are both also nationally known fine artists who have won numerous awards. Besides having their work in galleries and museum shows and selling limited edition giclées online they travel throughout the United States and Europe teaching oil painting classes. They enjoy traveling and teaching and it gives them extra income between sales. They have even linked up with art schools to take students out on painting excursions.

Kris Tualla - Author

Amazon bestselling author Kris Tualla writes historical romance fiction. She created several short video trailers as a way to publicize her books. You can find them on her website at www.KrisTualla.com.

Similar to a movie trailer, the book trailer is a short video that hints at the plot and entices the viewer to want to read more. This was such an effective sales tool that she realized it might be helpful to other authors to learn how to easily create them. She now teaches classes online on how to build an effective book trailer.

The classes are not only lucrative, but they also generate more interest in her novels thereby building her customer base. Because they are online classes she can conduct them from the comfort of her home, or anywhere else she might happen to be at the time.

Tualla also found there was a lot of interest in how to craft a novel, so she began teaching workshops at writer's conferences. Those workshops developed into a step-by-step informational book called *A Primer for Beginning Authors* that she sells on Amazon.com. Although creating a book is a slow process to steady cash, teaching classes based on the material you may currently be writing can generate quick money if you choose your venues well.

Cavin Gray - Actor

Award winning movie and TV actor Cavin Gray (www.CavinGray.com) teaches acting and improv classes one or two nights a week. He also offers private coaching to aspiring actors. It keeps his days free for auditions and allows him the freedom to cancel a class when he is called to go on a movie or commercial shoot. His students don't mind when a class has to be postponed, because as he advances his acting career the value of his classes increases.

Cavin has also learned other elements of the film industry so he finds work as a tech person on other people's projects as well. He has marketed his filming and editing skills to businesses and political campaigns and has made thousands of extra dollars each year from behind the camera while he continues to promote himself as an on camera actor.

He has even been contracted to produce a series of commercials for a major retail chain. While he is not in front of the camera for these commercials, his knowledge and expertise on the film set has given him the skills necessary to produce several commercials for a great freelance income. This "extra" money gives him the financial freedom to continue to pursue his acting career without becoming one of those "starving actors."

Keep in mind that the fastest money making ideas are services like teaching or consulting as opposed to creating and selling your creative products. That is because with selling a product you must first spend a great deal of time and money pulling together supplies and creating the painting or sculpture or movie. Then you need to find a buyer through ads, emails, sitting at art shows, applying to festivals etc.

As a creative it is essential to create those products to sell, but that is not a solution to raising FAST money. You need money from other sources *now* so you can promote yourself and your talents in the creative fields for future success. If you can teach a class or provide consulting services you can often get paid in advance or on the same day you teach the class.

So, begin by making a list of things you already know how to do that you could teach (even if only temporarily) to raise money quickly. Try to list twenty ideas.

Don't limit yourself to the obvious, either. Do you make a mean lasagna? Maybe you can teach a class to men on how to cook a meal for their significant others.

Do you have good Facebook skills? You can help businesses set up a Facebook account for their company. You can then charge a monthly fee to manage that account for them.

Don't worry at this point how you would get clients or if you think someone would pay you for that knowledge. Just get as complete a list as possible of all of the skills you have both in and outside the creative arts. You'll surprise yourself at how much you know!

Following is a list to start you brainstorming:

As an Artist You Can Teach:

- How to paint a mural for a child's room, family room or on a piece of furniture
- How to arrange a home's interior furniture and existing art pieces to maximize the beauty of the rooms, or Feng Shui consulting
- How to best display a sculpture and include a listing of resources for purchasing pedestals
- Art classes to children or adults at the local park and recreation centers or the senior centers
- Painting classes for the guests at a resort *(The resort should provide you with classroom space and a listing on their activities sheet. It makes the resort look better when they have more to offer their guests. You set the price and are paid directly by the guests.)*
- One-on-one painting or sculpting classes
- How teachers can inexpensively incorporate art into any curriculum
- How to plan and execute a solo art show
- How to turn your paintings into limited edition giclées
- How to find quality art shows or galleries for selling one's creative

pieces. You could include a listing of shows and their contact information.

- How to approach a gallery to display your art
- How to paint a sunset scene, or how to paint trees, or portraits, or even just water droplets
- How to choose, mat and frame watercolor paintings and include a list of inexpensive suppliers
- How to appreciate abstract or impressionist paintings
- How to find – and get - illustration jobs

As an Actor You Can Teach:

- How to act confidently in any situation (even if you're not)
- How to be persuasive when giving a speech
- Using basic improv comedy exercises to improve your workplace communication
- How to speak well in public
- Understanding body language and what you communicate without words
- How to select and edit pieces for an actor's demo reel
- What not to wear to an audition and why

- How to prepare for a cold read audition
- How to prepare for an improv show
- Rules of improv and how to use them
- Choosing a monologue for an audition
- How to get the attention of a casting director and is that the person you need to impress
- Image consulting, or how to wear colors to maximize your best features
- How to be memorable without blowing an audition
- Memorization techniques for learning scripts or giving speeches
- Acting for TV and film
- Acting for stage
- How to present yourself professionally during an interview

As a Film Maker or Photographer You Can Teach:

- How to photograph or videotape children like a professional
- How to dress for the best photo shoot ever
- How to use PremierPro, FinalCut, Photoshop, Avid or other programs
- How to create a pleasing composition

- How to photograph artwork or business products
- How to photograph a sunset scene or portraits that evoke an emotion
- How to create or find music to use in a video that is copyright free
- How Hollywood creates atmosphere and special effects
- How to create a trailer or video to advertise a book or service
- How to display photos creatively in a family memories book

As a Musician You Can Teach:

- How to play an instrument
- How to sing
- How to write a song
- Jingle writing
- How to record a CD
- How to create a music DVD
- How to book gigs
- How to develop a fan base
- How to use editing software
- How to use music effectively in the classroom to enhance learning
- How to use music with children who have physical or mental challenges

As a Writer You Can Teach:

- How to outline a novel
- How to plan a memoir
- How to break down your writing into bite sized pieces to create a book in 6 months or less
- How to write a children's book
- Website design, or offer to create a web page
- How to write a short personal biography
- How to write song lyrics for a special occasion
- How to create a Power Point presentation with "power" words
- How to become a better writer
- How to make believable characters
- How to write dialogue
- How to create cliffhangers
- How to market your book
- How to get media coverage for your book
- How to write great advertising sales copy
- How to better edit your own copy
- How to create a family legacy through writing

Once you decide on a class to teach that will generate fast money contact the park districts, local resorts, the Chamber of Commerce, acting studios, libraries, galleries, museums, schools, home school groups, businesses, art supply stores and even senior centers. Be sure to have a few different classes from which they can choose.

Park districts can be a great source of extra money for classes. The Park District will do all the advertising for you, but they will pay you an hourly rate (expect it to be around $25/hour + reimbursement for supplies.) They usually have a 4-6 month lead time from the time they book you to when you will actually be giving the classes, however, so you will need to plan and prepare well in advance.

Many libraries will not let you collect money from your audience, but often times the library has funds for special speakers. Ask if they have a speaker fee budget. Also, while you may not be able to sell things on site at a library you *can* mention your website and materials you have for sale there as long as it doesn't sound like a commercial for your products/services. You can also provide handouts to attendees that give all of your contact information.

Resorts will let you establish your own price, but you will collect the fees directly from the participants of your class. With each presentation you do, whether it is a class or workshop or lecture, be sure to have contact and biographical information about yourself to hand out. Think of your class as an additional venue for advertising your expertise. You might even get a few extra patrons for your work!

When you schedule a class post a note on Craigslist.com. Let your friends, family and business associates know about it through Facebook, EventBrite.com and emails.

When I announced that I would be teaching a series of drawing classes at the local park district some of my friends signed up. Another friend called and asked if I could teach a monthly class at her house for her daughter and several of her friends. Another woman asked if she could pull together a group of adult friends to have a "Wine and Watercolors" night that she would pay me to teach. She said she had no idea I taught art classes until she saw my announcement on Facebook. I brought in an extra $1000+ the first month.

The best classes are those showing people how to do something that is more difficult for the average person. For example, a class on how to design web pages or how to write a book proposal will likely get lots of students to attend.

One surprising benefit with these types of classes is that some of your students will prefer to pay you to do the project for them, even though you've just shown them how they could do it for themselves! They may still feel confused or would just rather pay you for your time and expertise instead of taking the time to do it themselves. This opens up the opportunity for you to do consulting or commission work for them and you can charge a premium price.

You may find that your Fast Money program is quickly turning into a freelance business. If so, *The Wealthy Freelancer: 12 Secrets to a Great Income and an Enviable Lifestyle* is a book you will want to own. The authors Steve Slaunwhite, Pete Savage and Ed Gandia teach you how to get clients, how to price your services and even how to create alternative streams of income so that you can make more money without taking more of your time.

Finally, whatever you decide to teach or whatever services you offer you must market them and yourself. *I'd Rather Be in the Studio: The Artist's No-Excuse Guide to Self Promotion* by Alyson B. Stanfield is an excellent guidebook that can help visual artists market their work.

"This one step - choosing a goal and sticking to it - changes everything!

- Scott Reed

4 Free Money

Okay, if you've followed the advice in the two previous chapters you have set aside some money for your creative project and you have brought in extra money from teaching what you know. Now you need that final "kick" to get it going. A few extra thousand dollars could make all the difference in bringing your creative dream to life, but where can you find people that will just hand you free money?

There are lots of books out there about getting funding through grants, but it is hard to find one that would be willing to fund exactly what you would like to do. You can put in a lot of time and research filling out forms and waiting several months only to find out your project was rejected and you'll receive no funding at all. You could then start the process all over again, but you need money more quickly than that.

Wouldn't it be easier to make your case about the value of your work if you could go some place where you could talk directly to the people who fund projects and let them hear your ideas and your passion? You know you could convince them that your project is worthy of their financial backing and begin to build a base of faithful patrons at the same time if only you were given the chance.

What if I told you there is such a place? Well, grab your sketchbook, your camera, your guitar, your script or your keyboard. There is a place where dreams come true and it's not Iowa (my apology to *Field of Dreams*).

In fact there are several places on the internet that all have a slightly different system and emphasis. These places are called crowdfunding sites. On these sites you can post your project where potential clients and patrons can see what you are trying to do and - if they like it - they will send you money to complete your project!

Crowdfunding sites can differ widely in their effectiveness and their guidelines for submission. Some are very limited in scope and are designed to promote only specific types of projects.

SellABand.com and PledgeMusic.com, for example, are specifically for musicians raising money for creating CD's and promoting their music or bands.

While the above sites are specific to a certain category of project, we are partial to the more general sites listed below. Instead of pinpointing one medium or specialty they are open to a variety of projects. Some even welcome raising money for charities or for personal medical issues. Because the projects are so varied, they tend to draw far more prospective funders for the projects.

Here, in alphabetical order, are just a few of the many general crowdfunding sites available:

GoGetFunding.com

IndieGoGo.com

Kickstarter.com

PeerBackers.com

RocketHub.com

All these sites have one thing in common. The more people who see what you post, the more money you are likely to raise.

Each site differs in how it works. Some charge a fee to post your project. Others help you raise money in exchange for stock or ownership in the profits of your business. All of them will take a small percentage of what you raise to keep the website functioning.

The artist decides on a project that he or she would like to pursue and determines the amount of money needed to accomplish that project. Armed with this information the artist posts the project online asking for people to sign on to the site pledging money to be a backer and bring the project to reality.

Movies, books, music CDs, sculptures, photography and painting exhibitions, original clothing designs, games and even inventions have all been funded through these portals to the creative universe. And in most cases it costs you nothing to post your project!

Now, just so we are clear on this, there have been numerous books, paintings, inventions, etc. that have *not* been funded on these sites as well. On Kickstarter, perhaps the most well known crowdfunding site, the rules state that the artist determines how much he or she wants to raise and how many days he or she will take to do it. If the artist does not receive the full amount needed by the final date specified, no funding is given.

Some sites let you keep all the money you raise even if you don't reach your full funding goal. These sites are called flexible funding sites. On IndieGoGo, for example, you receive all the money that is pledged to your project even if you do not reach your goal, but you pay an additional 5% penalty fee if your goal is not reached.

Flexible funding sites like IndieGoGo tend to raise less money overall. Flexible funding crowdfunding sites generally have a much lower percentage of projects that reach full funding as well, so consider carefully which type of site will give you the greatest chance of success.

So, how do you increase your odds of being one of those successful artists who receives full funding? You do your research, choose the most beneficial site, create the best possible presentation of your idea, tell as many people as you can about your project and follow the tips from someone who has been successful on a crowdfunding site.

We successfully used the crowdfunding site Kickstarter to fund the publishing of our children's book *Starfish on the Beach.* During our project launch we learned a lot about what works and what doesn't.

Regardless of which crowdfunding site you choose to use, these sites can work miracles in funding your creative project. It will take a lot of work and expertise on your part to reach your funding goals, but it is definitely possible to raise thousands of dollars to develop your creative expression.

How much money can be raised through crowdfunding sites? Kickstarter, for example, (founded in 2008) has been used to successfully raise hundreds of millions of dollars for creative artists of all kinds.

Kickstarter has become a favorite for the film industry in particular. In 2012 almost 10% of all films shown at the prestigious Sundance Film Festival received their financial backing through using Kickstarter. One movie project recently raised over $5 million in funding through Kickstarter!

In the remainder of this book we will walk you step by step through this amazing opportunity and share with you the insights we discovered to better insure your success.

There is a lot to learn and there are a lot of potential pitfalls along the way that can sabotage your plans but if you do the work, dedicate yourself to excellence in presentation, and have a great idea, this can be one of the most exciting things you will ever experience in your career – giving birth to an idea and seeing it come to life.

So, let's get started on the journey to making your creative dream a success story you can share for years to come.

Step One: Choose Your Project

Your first step is often more difficult than expected: decide on a project you want to bring to life. As a creative person there are probably several ideas you would like to pursue, but for now just pick one.

It is important that you choose something about which you are passionate, but something that isn't overly expensive to produce. If you are going to be successful in funding your project you will need to be able to communicate your passion to others and get them excited about your plans.

Here is a list of some ideas that other artists have successfully funded through various crowdfunding sites to get you started thinking about what type of project you want to pursue:

- Solo art shows featuring 30 or more paintings or photos for display and sale
- Children's books featuring original stories and artwork
- Coffee-table books featuring paintings or photography
- Limited edition prints or giclées to sell at shows or galleries or online
- Sculptures
- T-shirts and other pieces of clothing that feature original artwork or sayings
- Sci-Fi and Horror films
- Documentaries
- Original board games
- Books of poetry and novels, some illustrated with photos or illustrations
- A backyard musical that was written and staged for the local community
- Many different inventions, from unique camera tripods to a high quality ink pen for sketching

As you can see, the possibilities are only limited by your imagination and creativity. Select a project that excites you and get started. You may find as you get further into the following steps that you may need to modify your goals, but for now start with an idea and move forward.

Step Two: Determine Your Goals for a Crowdfunding Campaign

To determine whether you should even attempt a crowfunding campaign - and how to structure it - you need to determine exactly what you are hoping to accomplish. There are several questions you need to ask yourself before spending too much time developing a crowdfunding campaign.

1) Are you looking for some financial help to supplement your own resources or are you needing 100% help from others?

2) Are you simply hoping to gather a list of possible future patrons, even if the campaign itself isn't successful?

3) Are you looking to create a business for yourself or simply wanting to fund a single event or item? The answer to this question is an essential one to determine what type of campaign, if any, you should be pursuing.

4)Does your project fit a crowdfunding method of financing? If you are looking to buy land and a building for a gallery or museum, for example, you probably should be looking to more traditional financing venues like banks and the Small Business Administration.

5) How will your life change if you achieve your funding goals - or how will it change if you don't?

If you are looking to start a new career you need a lot of advanced planning before ever engaging in a crowdfunding campaign. Because a crowdfunding campaign can take several months to prepare and implement, is there a reasonable enough likelihood of success that the time invested will be worth it? If you are looking to start a business and your campaign fails you've just lost another 3-6 months of time that could have been better spent finding another career path.

6) Will your project be of sufficient interest to the general public to achieve the level of funding you are requesting? There are many great projects and ideas out there but their scope of interest is very narrow. They have too small of a niche to appeal to a broad group of people.

A consultant, for example, who wants to counsel teachers on how to address bullying issues in the classroom may have a hard time generating enough funding to pay for a national speaking tour on the subject. If they are writing a book about preventing bullying, however, they may find a broader market base and therefore be able to develop a successful campaign.

Remember, people will want to be convinced that you not only *should* succeed at this venture, but they must *want* you to succeed and be willing to trust that you will follow through with what you said you would do.

Your support from others will come from people who believe they will personally benefit by your campaign being successful. If they don't see any benefit to themselves they are very unlikely to fund your campaign.

You are making a promise to each backer that you will fulfill the rewards and work toward making your goal a success. Even in an all or nothing campaign people want to know that you are committed to seeing it through, that you have the ability to complete the project and that you have the integrity to be trusted with their support.

It is essential that you set definite, measurable goals so that you can best present your campaign to achieve those goals. Be clear in your own mind why you are embarking on this marketing challenge and what the consequences and benefits will be whether it fails or succeeds. This will help you determine whether a crowdfunding campaign will be the best venue for you to finance your creative project. You must be willing to decide to *not* run a crowdfunding campaign if it isn't a good fit and isn't likely to have a strong chance of achieving full funding.

Step Three: Determine How Much You Need

Once you know exactly what you want to create you need to determine all the expenses that you will incur to create it. Call or visit the suppliers that you frequent and get actual costs. This research is critical to your success or failure. Tally the amounts collected under a column entitled "Project Expenses."

Examples of what to include:

- Money for art supplies and frames to create a show*

- Fees to rent studio space
- Printing fees for posters, books, limited edition giclées, clothing or note cards featuring your work
- Travel fees and small, transportable painting supplies to create a series of paintings in another country*
- New camera lens required for a specific photography or film project*
- Costs for costumes or set designs
- A computer program necessary for your project, like FinalCut or Adobe
- Crew and equipment rental for a film
- Production costs for CDs or DVDs

**Caution: Many sites prohibit the use of the site to raise money to just buy equipment or to fund a trip. You can, however, include travel expenses and supplies as part of the total money you will need to complete a specific creative project.*

Step Four: Choose a Crowdfunding Site

Choose a site that best fits your project and preferences. If you choose one that costs you nothing to post your project then there is no financial risk to try it out.

You must also decide whether to post your project on a site that releases whatever funds you raise even if you don't reach your goal or go through an "all or nothing" site. A majority of the crowd-funding sites will only release the money if you meet your full funding goal in the time specified for your campaign.

There are pros and cons to each approach so be sure to do your research. You'll want to know what to expect and which approach will provide the likeliest chance of reaching your funding goal.

Make sure you read completely all of the rules of the site you are considering and follow them exactly. Rules can vary widely among sites and change frequently.

Failure to abide by the rules can have you banned from the site and your campaign suspended by the crowdfunding site. Make sure that you are comfortable working under the rules set out by the site before you begin setting up your crowdfunding site.

Service fees also vary significantly from site to site. Make sure you know how much those fees will be before you begin posting your project.

Step Five: Create Rewards That Will Motivate Your Backers

Up until now you have been thinking about what *you* want. Now you will have to think about what your patrons want. Depending on the project you choose, you will need to decide on rewards, or thank you gifts, to give to anyone who is willing to pledge to give money to your project.

These people are your backers. The rewards should be enticing enough to inspire the potential backer to put money into your project. You will need to keep in mind the cost of producing the rewards as well as the cost of your time to create them, however, and budget the cost of fulfilling these rewards into your total funding and scheduling needs.

This is a critical part of your crowdfunding project, so choose your rewards carefully. An ideal reward is something that is unique, but not expensive to produce (no more than 25% to 50% of the amount pledged). That way the money the backer pledges is going primarily into your project, not just buying the reward.

The ideal reward is also not time intensive to produce. A signed copy of your book, CD, DVD, or art print is perfect because the signing takes very little of your time and yet adds value to the item.

You will need to decide on a series of rewards that will correspond to the amount someone is willing to give you. These rewards should increase in value as the amount of the pledge increases.

The best way to illustrate how this works is to show you exactly what one artist did. Allison Torneros asked for $4000 and actually raised $8321 for a solo show! The following are the rewards she offered to anyone who backed her project.

$5 pledge: Backers name will be listed in the credits on her website under the listing of "Thank Yous to Sponsors."

$10 pledge: Backer will receive above reward plus a 5" x 7" print of one of her pieces.

$25 pledge: Backer will receive all of the above plus a T-shirt printed with a one-color graphic design.

$50 pledge: Backer will receive all of the above plus a signed 11"x17" poster print and handwritten thank you note.

$100 pledge: Backer will receive all of the above plus an original 8"x10" ink and acrylic drawing on paper (limited to 20)

$200 pledge: Backer will receive all of the above plus a super limited edition giclée print of one of the pieces from the show.

$500 pledge: Backer will receive all of the above plus a 12"x12" original painting on wood (limited to 5) and your name on wall decal at gallery under the list of supporters.

$800 pledge: Backer will receive all of the above plus a Paint By Word Project. "I will paint my interpretation of a single word of your choosing and include it in the show with your name listed under the piece. You will receive a single edition print of that piece.

$1000 pledge: Backer will receive all of the above plus a 24"x24" (limited to 5) piece from the show.

Now, let's analyze this list. The level at which Torneros received the most pledges was at

$25. That level received 39 backers. This meant she had to include the cost of producing and shipping 39 T-shirts to fulfill that pledge to her backers and 39 5"x7" prints. It cost her nothing to list their names in the "Thank Yous To Sponsors" credits on her website.

In almost every case the $25 - $30 pledge is the one that gets the most pledges. Whatever you offer at that level should have value and be enticing, but not be too expensive to produce and should not take much of your time to fulfill.

It was not until the $100 level that she offered an original. Some crowd funding sites allow you to limit the number of donors at a certain level*, so Torneros limited that reward to only 20.

The original was to be done on paper. Note that the piece would not be framed or matted to keep the costs of producing and shipping this reward low.

** Some sites now automatically limit all reward levels to a maximum number of supporters per reward level. Check your crowdfunding site's* *rules to see if they place a maximum limit per reward offered.*

Torneros received all 20 backers at that level. Once that limit was reached the site automatically closed that reward level. Just so you know, she received only one backer at the $1000 level and no backers at the $800 level.

Because choosing your rewards is critical to the success or failure of a project we will also analyze what a sculptor set up for his project.

Rainer Lageman's goal was to raise $3000 to place 25 metal sculptures randomly throughout Miami on the support columns of the Miami Monorail. Each sculpture depicted a person climbing and was made up of stainless steel squares and stars welded together. He exceeded his goal and raised $3585. His reward offerings were as follows:

$1 pledge: Backer receives a download of a map indicating the locations of all 25 sculptures on display.

$10 pledge: The map described above plus one stainless steel square like those used in the building of Climbers Over Miami.

$25 pledge: All of the above plus a Climbers Over Miami sticker

$50 pledge: All of the above plus a signed 8"x10" photo of one installed climber

$100 pledge: All of the above plus one signed and numbered print 20" x20" of one of the sculptures

$500 pledge: One of 13 body part sculptures

$9,900 pledge: One life size sculpture similar to the climbers installed throughout Miami

Again, the $25 pledge had the most backers. The $100 level had three, the $500 received one backer and the $9,900 reward was not picked up by anyone. My guess is that when people buy higher priced artwork they prefer to see exactly what they are getting.

Lageman's goal was to gain high visibility in his community. Even though he exceeded his goal of $3000, what he raised will barely cover his costs of sending out the rewards and installing all 25 sculptures. That's okay, since visibility and publicity was all he needed.

Lageman's sculptures were already completed and he did not need funding for materials. When he chose to go on a crowdfunding site with his project he was able to keep his goal amount very low as a result.

Ranier Langeman's campaign is a good example of how varied the reasons can be for initiating a crowdfunding campaign. Allison Torneros created a campaign specifically to make her art show possible. Langeman, however, simply ran his campaign to generate additional publicity. His rewards were paid for by his backers but he made very little additional money, if any. What he gained was a higher profile and awareness of his work and greater visibility.

You can also run a crowdfunding campaign as a way to presell your work. If you are running a crowdfunding campaign as a pre-sale the value of the rewards should be similar to what someone would have to pay if the product was being sold on the open market. You certainly need to factor in the site costs and the transaction costs that come with posting a campaign on the crowdfunding site, but in these circumstances your rewards should reflect a similar retail price of the item.

Here's how one artist used a crowdfunding campaign as a pre-sale of his work. Joshua Harker is a sculptor from Chicago who exhibits in galleries and at various shows. He figured out a way to economically create and duplicate elaborately designed sculptures with the help of technology.

For his project he created a small white human skull made of cut out filigree that he could easily duplicate using a 3D printer and a special type of plastic. It is much more complex than I will explain here. You can read about the process on his website:

www.JoshuaHarker.com

"The idea is to offer my work for a limited amount of time directly to the buying public without the extraneous exhibition costs & markups...a sort of pre-release," Harker said. "I will make as many as are pledged for in the next 45 days...be it one or a million billion. Assuming all goes spectacularly, I intend to offer all my work this way before it goes to a gallery or exhibition."

Harker set his goal very low - just $500. He zoomed way past his goal raising $36,000 when he still had 26 days to go before his project closed! This is a brilliant way to use a crowdfunding site if you have the type of project that would fit this approach.

Joshua created an item with good marketability that he could reproduce quickly. He built in the cost of each item adding a profit margin to each reward. He then used the crowdfunding site as his marketing arm.

The rewards Harker offered are as follows. We've included in parenthesis how many backers he received at each level.

$1 – a digital wallpaper of the skull for backer's computer (25)

$5 – a rotating 3D digital wallpaper of the skull (7)

$15 – a signed postcard plus the above rewards (4)

$30 – an 11" x 14" fine art print plus the above rewards (7)

$40 – a t-shirt featuring an image of the skull plus the above rewards (8)

$50 – small (2.6″ x 3.5″ x 3.5″) skull sculpture plus above rewards (620)

$100 – medium (3.7″ x 4.9″x 5″) skull sculpture plus above rewards (215)

$250 – large (5.25″ x 6.9″ x 7″) skull sculpture plus above rewards (46)

$500 – everything above plus an 11″ x 14″ fine art print on metallic paper, signed and numbered (8)

$750 – everything above plus an additional small skull sculpture in your choice of colors (4)

$1000 – everything above plus an additional medium skull sculpture in your choice of colors (1)

$1500 – everything above plus an additional large skull sculpture in your choice of colors (0)

Note: This artist is a sculptor so his backers wanted a sculpture (894 out of a total of 945 backers), but he found a way to offer one at a very low price ($50). He also made sure he could reproduce this sculpture quickly and economically without taking much of his own time.

Unlike preparing for a show or exhibition, Harker did not have to create the skulls in advance of putting his project up on the crowdfunding site. He had the money for all the skulls ordered before he created the first one. His crowdfunding site became a risk-free, online exhibition of his work, and a very successful one at that! At the close of this project Joshua Harker raised over $77,000! And if you will recall, he only had $500 as his original goal.

Harker now has initiated another crowd-funding campaign to release his latest work. It is a multiple piece sculpture and his rewards at lower levels include pieces of the complete work. He is an exceptional self promoter!

As you can see there are many reasons to run a crowdfunding campaign and the rewards should reflect the purpose of your campaign. You simply must find the balance between being too generous and too stingy with your rewards. What you offer in rewards should reflect the purpose of your campaign and the perceived value to your backers.

Step Six: Setting Your Crowdfunding Goal

So how much money should you set as your goal? Even if your crowdfunding site charges you nothing to post your project, if it is fully funded most sites take 5-10% for themselves. Also, because the funds are all run through credit sites like Amazon or Paypal there will be another charge of 3 - 5% for their services. You must include these service charges into your project funding goals.

Here is a summary of how to arrive at your money goal:

Write down the estimated amount of money you computed you would need in Step Three to complete your project.

Add the amount of expenses to create your backer rewards plus the estimated amount to ship each reward.

Total it.

Now add 10 to 15% more to cover both the crowdfunding site and Amazon or PayPal fees.

You could put that final total up as your goal, but there is one more piece of information you must keep in mind. On some sites, if you do not reach your goal in a set number of days (1 to 120) all pledges go away and you receive nothing, not even the emails of your backers.

We recommend that you don't try to "make money" with your posting. Instead, set the funding goal as low as possible to still raise the amount you need. The lower the goal the more likely it is you will reach full funding. Give yourself the best chance of being fully funded by being conservative in your funding goals.

Remember, there is no *maximum* limit to what you can receive. Many projects exceed their funding goals. You can raise more than you asked without penalty. Other than the processing fee for the payments that the site charges this is extra money right into your pocket to use as you wish. In 2011, 94% of the successful projects on one crowdfunding site exceeded their goals!

When we posted our *Starfish on the Beach* project we asked for $3800. We went over our goal, collecting $4085. A few people even contacted us through our website after the project was closed and sent checks directly to us to support the project because they wanted in on the rewards.

Greg Luzniak wrote and illustrated a children's book called *Three Goats Gruff,* an adaptation of the original story of a similar name. He wanted to produce a limited edition of 1000 signed and numbered hard cover books. His goal was $7500.

The crowdfunding site that he chose loved his project and made it a special feature resulting in his pledges going through the roof! He exceeded his goal by over $10,000 taking in $17,606! Very impressive and not typical, but it does happen.

Moral to the story: make sure you cover your expenses, but don't make the goal so high that you can't reach your goal and therefore lose all the pledges made. That said, if you are successfully funded you are required to fulfill all the rewards promised, so make sure you are not strapped with a project you must complete with insufficient funds.

If you choose to post your project on a flexible funding site remember you are still responsible to fulfill all of the pledges. Choose your crowdfunding site and rewards carefully to make sure you don't *lose* money on a poorly funded project!

Step Seven: Set Up Your Payment Site

You will need to set up a payment account with Amazon Payments or Paypal in order to receive funds from your backers. You will need to check with your crowdfunding site to see which payment options are available to you. Kickstarter requires an Amazon Payments account.

It is fairly simple to set up this account but it can take a few days for it to become operative. We recommend you do this early in the process so you can concentrate solely on developing your project from then on.

Amazon Payments functions similarly to Paypal. You can put money into the account to expedite online purchases, receive money from others, and manage your accounts almost like a bank.

Your backers will make their payments for supporting your project through the account you set up. If you are running an "all or nothing" campaign Amazon or PayPal will hold their donation amounts (depending on the crowdfunding site you choose) until you have reached your full funding. Once you are fully funded and your campaign has closed your crowdfunding site will notify Amazon or Paypal to process the cards and put the money into your account.

If you are running a flexible funding campaign donations will be processed upon submission and the money will either be held by the crowdfunding site or made available immediately in your Paypal or Amazon Payments account.

Even if you have the money available to you right away we recommend you do not take any of it until your campaign is completed. That way you are sure to have the money you need to fulfill all your backer's rewards.

Step Eight: Decide on a Deadline

You, the artist, decide how long you want to run your campaign, from 1 to 120 days. It is important to note that the majority of successfully funded projects ran for only 30 days. Longer is usually not better. However, you do need to give yourself enough time to get the word out to everyone you know.

We chose 40 days for our campaign and we were funded on the 39th day. We discovered that there was a flurry of activity at the beginning of the project because it was new and exciting to everyone who heard about it. At the end there was a sense of urgency that created another flurry of activity.

Every time we sent out an update of information on how the project was progressing we would see a bump in new backers. What was bad planning on our part was that we were gone for one week during the 40 day campaign. We hadn't realized how much daily monitoring the campaign would demand until we were into it.

Plan your fund raising campaign during a month when you can devote time to it every day and especially in the final week. That last week is crucial! You will need to send out additional emails or even make phone calls to friends and family to make sure your goal is met. Remember, for most crowdfunding sites your project is only funded if you reach your full monetary goal by the deadline.

Also be aware of the calendar. Are there holidays that will interrupt your fundraising project? Is it a month when lots of people will be on vacation or traveling? These issues can mean the difference between a successful funding effort and a failed one. Be sure to set your active crowdfunding window at a time that will reach the most people and that you can be actively involved in for the duration of the fundraising campaign.

The other thing you need to know is that when your campaign is over Amazon or Pay Pal can take up to 14 days to release the collected funds. Take that into account if you have a deadline to meet for your creative project. You don't want to miss the submission deadline of your film or miss the art exhibition because you couldn't get your money in time to complete the project.

To summarize:

Plan your campaign (we recommend 30 to 40 days). Realize that, depending on whether you are running a full funding or a flexible funding campaign, you may not receive any money from your successful campaign for up to two months past the start of the campaign.

Step Nine: Compose a Compelling Description of Your Project

This is the section where you get to describe your project in detail and why you want to raise the funds. This is your "sales pitch", so make it compelling without sounding like a used car salesman. Be honest and sincere, telling your story as to why this is important to you and why it should matter to your backers.

If you can include a story that shows why this project should be backed, include it here. Try to connect with your prospective backers. Many of them may be your friends and family, but our experience was that over 40% of our backers were people we had never met. They were friends or acquaintances of people we knew or people who simply came across our project when they were visiting the crowdfunding site. They became backers simply because they felt captivated by our story and wanted to be a part of this campaign.

Keep in mind that *you* may think this project is important, but if you can't convince enough backers to agree with you your campaign will fail. Emphasize what benefits your backers will receive as well as how your project will be of benefit to the community/state/country/world.

This is often where most people fail in their crowdfunding projects. If you are not good at writing promotional copy, hire someone to do it for you. At the very least, have an experienced copywriter review what you've written and edit it.

This is perhaps the most important step in the process, so dedicate as much time and expertise as you can to make sure you are communicating the value of your project to your prospective backers. You simply will not be successful if you can't convince others to support it with their money.

Step Ten: Create Your Video

If the descriptive copy you wrote from Step Nine is the "tell", then Step Ten is the "show". Just like show and tell when you were in elementary school, your written description and your video will work together to entice your potential backers to get involved.

Your video is where you get to show your stuff! You need to describe your project in all its glory. What do you envision and how will it enhance the lives of your backers and the world? You need to show your personality in the presentation so that the audience feels that they know who you are.

This is an essential part of your project that can determine your success or failure in reaching your crowdfunding goals. You need to show your potential backers important details about your project but also communicate why they should back it. Make it personal and create an emotional response in the viewer. They are more likely to back your project if you can tap into their emotions.

Remember, you will be introducing yourself to many new people who don't know you so make sure you put yourself in the best light possible. People support who they like and who they feel some affinity toward.

To illustrate this point, Tom and I recently coached Liliya, an artist, actor and writer, on her project. Seventeen years ago when she was barely a teenager her parents moved her from Russia to America. Her desire was to return to her homeland and write and illustrate a serious book about her impressions and memories.

Here in the United States Liliya is a stand-up comedian and improv actor. As her consultants we told her it was important that the viewers see the real Liliya with her passion and personality. We advised her to add some humor to her video which would make it far more compelling to potential backers.

If you are camera shy you might find the video portion of this process intimidating. Rest assured that many projects have received 100% funding even though the creators were never seen on the video. You are more likely to be successful if you *do* appear personally on the video, however.

If you choose not to show your face on the video you must make the video that much more compelling. People relate to other people, so by taking yourself out of the picture you must give them even more emotional reasons to support your project through stories and images. Don't sabotage your project by being camera shy unless you just can't do it.

Remember, this is not a beauty contest. People want to connect with you *and* your project, so let them see you communicate your passion for your project and they are more likely to back it.

So what should you include in your video? Your video should include visuals of your project or prior work if possible. Use the video to expand upon the description you put into words. By letting people see some of your work you will give them a sense of what to expect with your new project. If you are a musician you can include some clips from a few of your songs.

Be creative with your video and use it as a marketing piece for you and your talents. If it can stand on its own you might even want to consider posting it to Youtube or Vimeo for the duration of the campaign.

Think of yourself as one of your potential backers. What inspired your creative project? Did you struggle through a difficult time and emerge victorious? If so, tell that story. Others will relate to it. Were you inspired to do a film or photo essay of a small farming community that captured your heart, for example? Explain that and show a few of your photos. Grab your potential backer's emotions and you'll likely gain access to their wallet as well.

Greg Luzniak was inspired to create *The Three Goats Gruff* children's book when he became a father for the first time. He rewrote the story to make it reflect a family of three; Mom, Dad and baby goat. His rich illustrations drew people in to read more about the project and his personal family information touched hearts and helped to clinch the deal.

Many years ago Tom's brother and wife adopted three children from difficult home situations. We have watched them through the years as they have struggled with discouragement and doubts as to whether or not they were doing enough for these children as their needs were so great.

This was on our minds as we created our children's book, *Starfish on the Beach*. We wanted it to be a book that would not only delight children with its story and watercolor illustrations, but we wrote it to be an encouragement to the parent/guardian who reads it out loud to their child as well.

Our story, inspired by *The Star Thrower,* an essay by Loren Eiseley, tells of a mom and daughter who at low tide discover starfish stranded on a beach. The two set out to rescue the starfish from dehydrating in the sun by tossing them back into the water.

After a time the mother, seeing the vast number of starfish that need their help, tells her daughter, "I don't think we're making much of a difference here." In response the child tosses in one more starfish and replies, "I made a difference for that one!"

We have found that although it was created to be a children's picture book, the story resonated with adults as well as children. Teachers, parents, volunteers and people who simply were trying to make a difference in this world were moved by the story. Many chose to back the project so they could get a book to give as a gift of encouragement to someone else.

Teachers are also now using it in their classrooms to teach compassion and civic responsibility to their students. As a result of its universal message of encouragement, *Starfish on the Beach* reached #1 on the Amazon Best Seller list in its category! This would not have been possible if we had not been able to raise the funds to produce the book.

Another catalyst for creating *Starfish on the Beach* was our involvement in volunteering for a charity that touched our hearts. It is called the Pajama Program and has taken on the massive task of trying to give a children's book and a pair of pajamas to each child being rescued from a dangerous home situation.

We knew we wanted to support this important work in any way possible. When we put our project up on a crowdfunding site we mentioned this charity and that we would be donating the first books off the press to that program.

Several individuals that became backers to our project told us that they had adopted their children or had been raised in a foster home themselves and immediately felt a rapport with what we were trying to doing. It was that little piece of information that motivated many of our backers to pledge to support the project. *

Others had different reasons to back the project. A few told us they lived near the coast and became backers because they loved the watercolor beach scenes. Other backers told us that they were grandparents and signed up at the level that would give them enough books for all their grandchildren.

Bottom line: Show a piece of your heart and you will find others who will relate to what you are trying to do.

** A note of caution: Most crowdfunding sites prohibit their sites from being used solely as a fund raiser for charities and non-profits. They are only to be used for funding creative endeavors. A few sites are open to charitable fund raisers, however. Be sure you do your research before posting your site. You don't want to be kicked off the site and have your project refused for violating the site's rules.*

You might never be allowed back on that site if you violate their terms, so read their guidelines thoroughly and follow them to the letter. Because Starfish on the Beach *was not being produced solely as a fundraiser for a charity it did not violate the rules of the site.*

Preparing the Video

When you set up your video camera to describe your project have a script or an outline to keep you on track. Be creative. Add visuals, and show some of your creative work if possible. If you are an artist, for example, a time lapse video of you creating your artwork would be an excellent addition. People love to see a work of art evolve right before their eyes.

For writing projects, include royalty free photos of places in your story or other visuals that relate to your written project. For musicians, include some of your music in the background. Film makers can show brief clips from other projects they've been involved in or relate some basic story line.

Regardless of which type of artistic project you are proposing, add visual elements that relate to your project. You can add music in the background if you want, but do not use copyrighted music. The site will take down your project if you do.

Show your passion. Why is this project important to you? Like Tom and I, did a friend or family member's plight inspire you? Did you experience something you need to express? Do you have an opportunity that you want to seize, but can't without the funding?

Make your video as good as possible but don't worry if your video isn't slick and professional. People are moved to respond when you are personal and honest. Simply show and tell why this matters to you so that your project will matter to the people who are hearing about it.

You will want to write a different script for your video than you have for your description. Don't just recite the same text as is printed in your description. Your video should give more information than the description you write about the project. The viewers will see both the written description and the video, so give them a reason to watch.

The video script can contain most of the elements of the written description but should include additional information as well. Tell a story in the video, for example, or show things that can't be described well in text. The video gives you some additional ways to communicate so take advantage of the options that video provides.

Some of the most compelling projects and videos are often chosen to be featured as hot projects on the crowdfunding website. If you are one of the fortunate ones to have your project featured by the crowdfunding site, your funding will skyrocket!

This is worth gold to you, so don't skimp on the video. Be creative, expressive, and compelling with the use of music, images, humor, and heart. In short, be bold, be unique and be memorable.

Step Eleven: Compose Your Biography – Why You Are the One to Create This

Your biography is more important than you may think. It is not a resume, nor is it necessary to include all your training or your job history. Only include the information that answers the following questions:

- Why are you the right person to create this project?
- Why would someone want to pledge to back your project?

- How can they find out more about you, the artist?

It is more important to tell some things about yourself and how someone can contact you than it is to tell about your previous jobs or education. If your work experience or education helps to answer the above three questions, however, then feel free to include it.

The purpose of your biography is not to impress people with how knowledgeable you are. Instead, it is simply a way for potential backers to get to know you better and gain confidence in your ability to produce a quality product or service. When people are comfortable about who they are supporting they are more likely to back your project.

It is also important that you let people know of other creative projects you've been involved in. If possible you should include visuals in your video of clips of some of these other ventures.

Unfortunately, there have been some scammers on crowdfunding sites, especially on the flexible funding sites who simply take the money and are never heard from again. People will trust you more if they have proof of prior work and can feel some assurances that you will fulfill your rewards and complete your project.

A Word About Websites

It helps to have a website to which you can refer people, but a website is not required for your success. Websites offer another way for people to learn more about you and your creative work, however. They also provide a second layer of security to your prospective backers that you are a legitimate artist with a following. It creates a higher level of trust in those who may not know you and helps them feel more comfortable about pledging money to your campaign.

We had several people find our project by going to our website after the fund raising campaign was over. They wanted to buy *Starfish on the Beach,* our children's book, and were able to find us because we had a website:

PeaksPublishing.com

They were able to learn more about us and our other books at the site as well. Many visitors to our site then went on to purchase *Starfish on the Beach* either directly from us or through other sources like Amazon.

We even had some people contact us about having Lindy do some illustration work for their projects. Without the website we would never have known about their interest and they might not have ever purchased the book. Our website has resulted in several more patrons since our Kickstarter project closed.

If you are not comfortable with creating your own website you can hire someone to create a simple one for you. There are also some simple tutorials available for free or at very low cost that can coach you through setting up a simple website.

The easiest way to set up a website is by using Wordpress. They have hundreds of website templates you can set up for free. You simply put in your own personalized content. You can sign up for your own free website builder at:

Wordpress.org

There are two other things you will need if you want a website. First, you will need a domain name. That is what a website's web address is called. For example, PeaksPublishing.com is the domain name for our publishing company.

The other essential component to setting up a website is a hosting company. We recommend HostGator (hostgator.com). You can have your Wordpress website hosted through Hostgator for as little as $5/month. If you go to Hostgator and sign up for your hosting first they have a very simple Wordpress download button that makes installing Wordpress on your computer a breeze. You can even purchase your domain name through them.

You can also get your domain name from other companies like GoDaddy.com and other sources as well. Shop around for the best deal on domain names. All companies that offer them for sale can get any domain you want that hasn't been taken by someone else. Only the prices and "extras" differ among all the companies that offer them for sale, so it will pay to shop around for the best prices and options.

Obviously, it is well beyond the scope of this book to provide detailed instructions on setting up a website. If you would like step by step instructions on how to set up a website and use it to create an online business for your work, visit:

www.CashForCreatives.com

We will have a 63 video course available that will show you everything you will need to know to set up an online business for your artistic pursuits. This course covers all the "technical" aspects of how to set up and implement a website to develop your business online.

Simply click on the *Resources* tab at the website. There will be several additional resources there as well which you might find useful to further your creative business.

"Success is as much about the courage to attempt something as it is about the outcome. You can never achieve success if at first you don't try."

- Tom Schneider

5 A Successful Launch: Making Your Crowd-funding Project Fly

Once you have your video uploaded onto your crowdfunding site, your rewards posted and your biography and description just the way you want it you are almost ready for your launch. Mark the official launch date on your calendar.

A few days before the official launch of your project take some time to share the site with a few close friends. Have them view your proposal and read it through. Ask them for feedback. If they like what you're doing ask them if they would be willing to make a pledge the first day of the launch to get you started. If they have any suggestions that you think have merit, make the changes on your site.

Gather any lists that you have: friends, family, and patrons. Review every aspect of your proposal one more time to look for typos, errors, or omissions. Then, when you are happy with what you are offering, LAUNCH! It will be scary to put yourself, your passions and your creative work out there, but it is essential that you follow through and push that launch button.

Notify everyone that you have launched a campaign on a crowdfunding site and that you would appreciate their support. Put your campaign link up on Facebook and send it to friends through email.

For those folks that don't use a computer much, send them a letter about your project. They can send you a check that you can hold until the project goes through. Ask another friend to post that check amount on your site so that your project will get credit for it and push you closer to your goal. You can sign the pledge check over to your friend that posts it.

IMPORTANT: You CANNOT fund your own project. If you are close to reaching your goal it may be tempting to just log on to pledge the last $100. The payment company or the website itself will block you and if it detects that you have opened a new account in a different name to fund your own project it will shut you down completely. Don't try it!

If you have a large number of Facebook or email friends you have a huge advantage. However, do not be discouraged if you do not. Tom and I together had a list of about 250 people when we launched our Kickstarter project, which is not a very large list. We asked each person on our list to send our information on to their friends if they liked what we were doing and so our circle was greatly enlarged.

Not everyone will post your information on their social networks, but those that do are basically endorsing your project and giving it even more credibility. It doesn't take very many people to boost your numbers significantly. If only 10 people forward your campaign information on to their list of 250 friends you will be reaching another 2500 people with notification about your project!

Now you may be tempted to sit back and watch the pledges come in. After all, you've been working on this project for months now!

Don't allow yourself to slack off at this point. This is the home stretch! It is vital that you contact someone every day about your project. Make every email and Facebook message personal to the recipient. You only have 30 or 40 days, so dedicate yourself to politely but enthusiastically marketing your crowdfunding website.

Tell people about your project over coffee or while out watching your son's baseball game. Keep the code or URL of the link to your project with you at all times. Someone may say, "I would love to see your project." You will be able to give them the URL for them to log on and see what you have posted. You can even show them your video on your phone.

Your crowdfunding site will notify you by email every time someone pledges to your site. It is important that you thank EVERY backer as soon as possible after you are notified of their pledge. This is someone who believes in you or what you are doing!

Also, ask them if they would send information about what you are trying to do on to their friends, reminding them that if you do not reach your goal by the specified date the project may not happen. Email them the link that they can copy and paste to make it easy for them to share your information.

Keep sending updates to everyone you know on Facebook and through emails and Twitter as your project progresses, but don't spam. We notified our friends of how our project was doing about once a week unless there was a specific reason to contact them more often.

Reaching certain milestones along your fundraising journey is a great excuse to send out another email with thanks and encouragement. People will appreciate hearing from you whenever you reach certain benchmarks, i.e. "We just reached the 30% mark toward attaining our goal and we still have 28 days to go!" or "We just raised our first $1,000. Only $3,000 more to go!"

When you reach your full funding, celebrate! Send out a "we did it" email so everyone can share in the joy of seeing your dream become reality. Remember, they supported this project so they wanted you to succeed. They want their rewards, too!

There are still a few things you'll have to wait for before you can start implementing your dream, however. First, no money will be processed until your project timeline expires. Even if you get full funding in the first few days you'll have to wait until the end of the term before any money will be processed. This allows even more backers to join in supporting your cause so you can exceed your goal.

Secondly, it can take 7-14 days after the close of your project for the funds to be processed and made available for you to access. Remember, both your crowdfunding site and Amazon Payments or Paypal will take their share out of what you have raised in support of your project.

Finally, you are likely to have one or two of your backers whose cards don't process properly. Sometimes they are simply over their limit. In other cases they entered in their card number or other information improperly. In any case, you may need to contact those backers whose cards did not process to let them know there was a problem. In most cases it is easily remedied. This again can take some time to resolve, however, and will tie up those funds until they are processed.

What if my Project Does Not Reach Full Funding?

One of the questions we are asked most often is, "What happens if my project does not get fully funded?" This depends on which crowdfunding site or option you chose for your campaign. If it was a full funding "all or nothing" site you do not receive any of the money pledged. The crowdfunding site labels the project as unfunded and the backers' credit/debit cards are not charged. You can rework the project, improve it and re-post it to try again later if you wish.

If you choose a site that allows you to receive all funds pledged regardless of whether or not you reach your goal (flexible funding), you may be in a situation where you must fulfill the promised rewards with a minimal amount of funds needed to do it. This may not leave you much if any money left to fund the project you desired. You will most likely be charged a higher processing fee as well by the crowdfunding site as a penalty for not reaching your funding goal.

Why Some Projects Fail and How To Make Sure Your Project is Not One of Them

There are many reasons that more than half of the projects posted on crowdfunding sites do not receive their full funding. We often look through the pending projects and usually have been able to accurately predict which projects will succeed or fail just by what the artist has posted. What we cannot predict is how much the artist will work toward the success of his or her project. Here are just some of the many reasons why a particular project may fail to reach its funding goal.

1) Choosing the Wrong Crowdfunding Site

As mentioned earlier, every crowdfunding site has a unique emphasis. Spend some time on each prospective site looking at the types of projects posted and which categories have the highest percentage of fully funded projects.

For example, IndieGoGo is one of the largest crowdfunding sites. In addition to the usual creative categories, however, it offers categories for raising funds to pay for medical bills, money for sending kids to camp and other non-creative projects. Because Indiegogo accepts virtually any project in any category you are competing for attention with tens of thousands of other projects. Unless you are a highly accomplished marketer or have a truly compelling project you are likely to simply get lost in the crowd.

Relatively few projects are fully funded on this site compared to some other sites. The success rate for fully funded projects on Indiegogo stands at about 28% as of the writing of this book. This percentage is for *all* categories combined. For creative projects it is often much lower. While films do fairly well on this site, virtually no books receive full funding, for example.

If you choose to use Indiegogo as your crowdfunding site for a creative project you will need to design your campaign so that it will stand out from the crowd. If you need full funding for your project this is probably not the best site for you, in our opinion.

The main reason many people choose sites like Indiegogo for their crowdfunding campaign is because they have the choice of choosing either a flexible or a fixed spending option. This may be an acceptable option if you can use whatever money comes in, even if you don't receive full funding for your project. Just remember you will lose over 10% of what is pledged in Indiegogo fees and transaction fees. You'll also have to fulfill any rewards you promised to your backers. Make sure you aren't losing money on this type of campaign if you don't receive adequate funding.

Kickstarter is our preferred crowdfunding site because it is focused exclusively on raising funds for creative projects. It also has had the most success in fully funding projects. Kickstarter is a full funding site only. This means if you don't reach your fundraising goal you receive nothing.

As of the writing of this book 42% of the campaigns posted on Kickstarter received their full funding. This is down almost 6% from one year ago - perhaps a reflection of our difficult economy. It could also be that more people are posting projects without having fully planned and properly presented their idea to achieve the necessary support.

Don't let those statistics discourage you. Just make sure you do the work necessary to make *your* project a success. Have a great idea, do the background work to set up your campaign properly and offer great rewards. Then market your campaign effectively and you'll be part of that 42% of fully funded campaigns.

Check out several crowdfunding sites carefully before you decide where to post your project and focus your efforts. Any of them can bring you success, but one may be more suitable for your project than another. The site you choose must provide you with the best opportunity to see your project funded. Your success will come from both the work you put into promoting your project and from where you choose to host it.

To help you determine which crowdfunding site will work best for you, ask yourself the following questions:

1) Is my project for a creative pursuit or for personal needs like rent, etc.? Make sure you read the site's guidelines for submissions

thoroughly to know whether your funding needs are a good match for the site.

2) Can I fulfill my goals if I only get partial funding? You should only list a goal as high as necessary to fund your project. Will you be able to achieve at least some of your goals if you only receive partial funding?

3) Can I produce the rewards even if I don't receive full funding? Your rewards must be met even if you only have a few backers if you choose to go with a flexible funding campaign.

4) How many potential backers do I need to reach to achieve my funding goals? Remember, the average backer pledges $25 or so. Run the numbers and see how many people you need. Then determine if that is reasonable and matches other successful projects with similar funding needs on the site.

5) How unique is my project, and will it stand out from other projects on the site? You need to be on a site that has successfully funded other projects like yours. You also need to position your project to be something that is different than others currently on the site.

6) What percentage of the funding will go to the crowdfunding site, especially if I don't reach my full funding goal? Some sites charge almost double the fees if you don't reach your goals. You must factor this in to your fundraising needs.

7) Is my project a good fit for the crowdfunding site - are there other similar type projects on the site? You don't want to put an invention project on a site that lists mostly book projects, for example.

8) What percentage of all projects reached full funding on this site? Even in sites that will give you all the money raised without full funding you need to know what your chances are of getting all you need to reach your goal.

9) Have other projects similar to mine reached full funding on this site? You should research several of the past projects listed on the site and see how many were fully funded.

10) How long has the site been in existence? Generally the longer the site has been up the more potential backers are aware of it. The more popular sites can sometimes give you a better chance of people outside your own

specific contact lists finding you and supporting your project.

11) How many projects are listed on the site, and how many visitors does the site get? You may be tempted to run your campaign on a small site with fewer projects since yours will have a better chance of standing out. The problem is that if no one is going to that site you are relying exclusively on your own contacts to fund your campaign. You are not likely to get a lot of "browsers" who come across your campaign and choose to support it if no one is coming to the site except people you know.

When we ran our successful campaign for our children's book almost 30% of our backers were people we had never met. Many of those were people who just happened upon our project while they were browsing the site and were touched by our story, artwork and message. This can mean the difference between success and failure. In our case, we would not have reached our full funding goal without these "browsers."

That's why it is so important to have a compelling story to tell. You never know who may stumble upon your site and be moved to contribute. Two of these "browsers" contributed $100 to our campaign!

When choosing your site look for both the number of total projects in your category and the percentage of projects that received full funding. The more projects that are listed in your category and the higher the percentage of fully funded projects, the better the fit.

2) Not Getting Approved To Post Your Project

Before anything else is done you must convince the crowdfunding site that your project is one that they should allow. Some sites require prior approval before you can post your site. Many projects slip up here and do not receive approval to move forward. Others will take any project with few exceptions and don't have a pre-screen approval process. You must thoroughly read through the terms and conditions before submitting your idea to see if your project meets the requirements of the crowdfunding site.

When we consult with our clients we give them a 100% money back guarantee that if they follow our advice their crowdfunding site will give their project the green light. No one can guarantee full funding, but you won't get anything if you can't first get your project accepted for listing!

3) Choice of Project

Some artists choose a project that has an extremely limited market interest. For example, one teacher who works with special needs children found she had great success with her students by incorporating art projects. Her students created delightfully unique drawings that she wanted to compile into a book and produce.

She put her idea up on Kickstarter but was unable to raise even 20% of her needed goal. If she had expanded her book to include information on how parents and teachers could achieve the kind of success she did with special needs children and used the drawings as illustrations she may have had a better response. Remember that people highly value information. The drawings were delightful, but by themselves they had little market value.

4) Poor Follow Through

Tom and I discovered a project on one site that we decided to back. The art was well done, though we were concerned that the goal was set too high. Because we like to help other creatives live their dreams we often back other projects. In fact, when we take on a Cash For Creatives coaching client we commit to backing their project with a $100 pledge.

This artist that we backed, though she was *not* our client, made a big mistake. She never communicated with us and we can assume she never communicated with any of her other backers. We never even received a thank you email for pledging money to her project. Neither did we receive any updates on how the project was progressing.

That was a big mistake! Needless to say this project also failed. Other backers probably felt taken advantage of and unappreciated as we did so they were not willing to share information about this project with their lists.

Keeping your backers informed and excited keeps them telling others about what you are doing. Remember, your backers sign on because they want to see your idea become reality. In most cases they want to own a piece of that success through the rewards.

If you don't receive full funding your backers also do not receive their piece of the pie on a full funding site. This motivates them to "sell" your project to their friends and family, but they need to be kept informed and know they are appreciated.

This is one of the most important components of a successful project. A simple email of thanks will go a long way toward not only keeping your backers happy but also encouraging them to tell others about your project. When they are invested emotionally as well as financially in your project they will put more effort into helping you reach your funding goal.

5) Threshold Price Too High

It is important that you not set your money goal too high. You must be able to cover your expenses to be able to create your project and fulfill the rewards, but if the price threshold seems unreasonably high the viewing public will be less motivated to sign up to help it succeed.

Your funding goal should match the perceived value to the audience. The higher the funding goal the more substantial the rewards must be and the greater value potential backers must find in seeing your project succeed.

Remember, people are parting with their hard earned money to support your idea. Make sure it is presented in a way that will give them the assurance that it is worth the investment. Let them know in your video or description what the money raised will be used for.

Sometimes this value is found in how much "skin" you have in the game. For example, award winning film director Paul DeNigris set out to create *Parallax,* a movie short inspired by the true story of an American soldier and his encounter with an Iraqi national. He set aside $2000 of his own money for the film project and mentioned that fact on his crowdfunding site. His goal was to raise the additional $8000 he would need to create the film and to enter it into film festivals.

Parallax was fully funded and went over its goal, raising a total of $9,350. If Paul had asked for the full $10,000 it may have been too much to reach and all funding would have been lost. He also might never have reached his goal if he hadn't mentioned that he was putting some of his own money into the project.

Knowing that the film maker himself had saved up a significant amount of his own money to make the movie was inspiring to the backers and gave an assurance to them that the artist would do what had to be done to complete the project.

You can watch the trailer for *Parallax* at www.ParallaxTheFilm.com. In 2012 *Parallax* won Best Arizona Short in the Phoenix Film Festival. The film went on to be presented at the 2012 Cannes Film Festival in the Short Films Corner. *Parallax* was also recently featured in the Hollywood Shorts Film Festival and it all began on a crowdfunding site!

6) Not Offering Appropriate Rewards

You need to put a lot of thought into your rewards and make them as inspiring and imaginative as your project. Realize that there are different backers with different financial resources. A poorly thought out rewards program is almost guaranteed to result in a failure to reach your funding goals.

As an example, one artist hoped to simplify the whole process by offering only a single reward. She stated that anyone who pledged $10 or more would receive her illustrated book with a personal note. Apparently this inspired very few people because she raised less than 5% of her goal.

7) Lack of Marketing Knowledge

Each of us makes decisions on whether to buy or not buy something. The same is true in whether someone will be motivated to support your campaign. It is essential to understand *why* someone would choose to support you.

Identifying all the possible reasons someone would choose to support your campaign is one of the most important things you need to determine if your campaign is going to be successful.

Most people do not decide to purchase something based on a making a logical choice. Instead, they usually buy for emotional reasons. The purchase will make them happier, make their lives easier, or will provide them with some other emotional benefit. You must present your project in such a way that you tap into people's emotions. There may be good logical reasons for them to participate, but if you don't tap into their emotional side you're not likely to motivate them enough to get involved.

This is perhaps the most difficult part of running a crowdfunding campaign, and it will take a great deal of time to get your video and description copy "just right" to provide a balance between information and an emotional "tug". If you come across too sappy or dramatic you'll turn people off from supporting your campaign. If you don't engage their emotions at all you end up with the same result.

Unless you have some experience at writing good marketing copy you should probably seek out someone with expertise in that area and ask them to help you create the description and the video text for your campaign. We believe that this is one of the primary reasons that many campaigns don't reach their funding goals. They simply don't touch the hearts of those viewing their campaign.

Don't neglect this important part of your campaign! It is critically important to your success.

8) Poor Presentation

One project that should have been able to receive full funding hit their final day having only received 25% of what they needed and was stamped as unsuccessful. The project was being produced by film makers who had a lot of experience and connections in the industry.

The film makers were asking for $20,000 which is quite low for a full length movie. They even had several backers who pledged above the $250 level. One pledged $1000. They offered a wide range of creative rewards from DVDs and t-shirts to walk-on roles in the movie.

So what went wrong? In trying to gain attention and draw people to their site they titled their project "This Movie Sucks!" Apparently people believed them and didn't waste their time checking it out further.

Don't play games with the title or description of your project. This is serious business! You can be funny, playful or tell a compelling story in presenting your project (and generally you will have more success in reaching your goal if you do) but beware of those subliminal messages you are including in your proposal.

Remember, your goal is to raise the funds needed to bring your creative dream to reality. Make sure the message you are sending out is taken seriously and presents your project in a positive light. Unfortunately for these successful filmmakers they had a great idea for a movie but didn't understand much about marketing!

"Creativity is as complex as the universe and as simple as propping up a window with a ruler."

- Tom Schneider

6 Why Take the Risk?

Now that you have learned about crowd-funding you should have a pretty clear picture of whether you have a project that would fit this funding model. It's up to you to determine whether this is something you are willing to take on.

Most creative people suffer from insecurity. After all, you pour your heart and soul into your craft - what if people don't like it? What if you feel you've done a fantastic job but you don't get the sale or the contract? What if you put your best effort into a crowdfunding campaign and don't get the funding you need?

Rather than asking, "What if my project fails?" the better question is, "What do I gain by trying?" The truth is there is almost all upside to running a crowdfunding campaign and very little downside other than a slightly bruised ego. Let's take a look at some of the additional ways you can benefit from a crowdfunding campaign even if it is not successful financially.

Build a List of Potential Patrons

If you run a crowdfunding campaign you will find out who your most loyal current clients are because they will support your project. You may also pick up several additional followers who find out about your campaign through your supporters posting the information about your campaign on their emails or social media sites.

While you won't get the emails for these potential supporters in most "all or nothing" crowdfunding sites you can still send a bulk email to the group letting them know *your* website or email information. Ask them to contact you so you can keep them informed about future projects or events. Most of them will gladly reply and give you permission to contact them. After all, they were interested enough in what you were offering to support it!

Also, if you have a website, you can direct them to your website where they can stay updated on your other activities. You will find virtually all of your would-have-been supporters will want to stay in touch.

Pre-sell an Item

Many crowdfunding sites have been set up to simply pre-sell a product. You may have a creative item that can be reproduced in variable quantities. You can set a very low financial goal for your crowdfunding campaign so you are virtually guaranteed of receiving full funding. All backers will then be rewarded with one of several items you can give them one at a time.

While this doesn't work as well for printed items like limited edition prints or giclées unless you have already printed them, it does work well for things like pottery, reproducible sculptures or other items that can be manufactured or printed one at a time. Also, any downloadable items can fit well within this type of campaign since there is no physical product that needs to be created and shipped.

Many artists have found great success with these kinds of campaigns. They are simply pre-selling the items and will fill the orders based on the demand. Just make sure you can produce these items fairly quickly and in sufficient quantities to fulfill all the rewards required.

Test Market a New Business or Item

Crowdfunding campaigns can be an excellent test marketing tool for many projects. Let's say you want to see what the demand might be for a cookbook on 101 ways to make healthy donuts. (By the way, if you can come up with this, I'll buy it! They are Tom's favorite vice.)

While you should have the basic recipes and a general outline of how the book will be created, you do *not* have to have the book completely written and ready to go to press! Simply create an all or nothing crowdfunding campaign and make your case for healthy donuts. Then spread the word like any other crowdfunding campaign and see how many supporters you can get.

Set your goal high enough so that if there is sufficient interest you can actually produce the book and fulfill the rewards. Then, if you reach your goal, you know you have a hit on your hands and you can complete the book.

If you are going to run a crowdfunding campaign as a test market make sure you mention in your campaign that delivery of rewards will happen x number of months into the future after the completion of the campaign. This should be no more than 4 months, and should be less if possible. You don't need to mention the book isn't written yet and that this campaign is a test market, but you don't want people thinking they will get a book three weeks after the close of the campaign either.

Set realistic expectations for your backers and for yourself. Don't make promises you can't deliver! When you are up front about how soon they can expect their rewards you won't have any disgruntled backers. If they don't want to wait that long they won't become a backer.

Raise Some Money

A majority of crowdfunding campaigns never reach their goal of full funding. While we greatly prefer the all or nothing sites for most projects, there are times when *any* money coming in will be of help. As long as you can fulfill any rewards required for your backers based on how much is contributed these flexible funding campaigns can be of some value.

Even if you don't receive full funding, you have made many more people aware of your work. If you include a website address in your biography you may still gain new patrons and fans. The backers who believed in your project may still be interested in purchasing something else from you in the future. You make a little extra money and have the satisfaction of knowing you were bold enough to put yourself and your talents out there.

If you do not put your project up on a crowdfunding site you are guaranteed not to receive funding. However, if you put in the effort to put your best work forward you may be like the nearly 40% who receive all their funding and can boldly move ahead. You may even be like Tom and I and exceed your goal!

Create Forward Momentum

One final reason to create a crowdfunding campaign is that it generates forward motion. It gives you, the creative, an opportunity to present yourself in a new way. It teaches you to create a plan, how to follow through on that plan, and hones your marketing skills. Even a failed campaign becomes a learning experience and you'll be better at marketing your work as a result.

If you don't receive full funding spend some time re-evaluating every aspect of your campaign to see where you could have made it better. Was the video compelling enough? Did the description tug at the reader's heartstrings? Were the rewards strong enough? Was the concept one that would have a broad enough market base?

Don't be afraid of asking some of your friends who *didn't* support your campaign why they didn't. Don't make them feel guilty. Let them know you sincerely want to learn something about this campaign. You genuinely want to know why they didn't feel motivated to support it. By asking for their honest replies you will gain some insight into how to improve upon future campaigns.

BE HUMBLE! You don't want to lose friends by coming across as complaining or accusatory. If they know you are asking purely for informational purposes and not to put a guilt trip on them they will be more open to give you their honest opinion.

Some reasons may have nothing to do with the project itself. If your project was a children's book and they don't have children you shouldn't be surprised if that's the reason they give you for not supporting the project.

Your project won't appeal to everyone. If they tell you they didn't like the illustrations, however then add that to your list. If you find several people making the same comment, you've learned something about how to improve upon future projects.

To be a successful artist or creative you must also be a diligent and successful marketer. Working on a crowdfunding project will train you how to market yourself. It will also show you where your strengths and weaknesses are.

If people didn't find the video particularly interesting you might want to link up with a professional video person for future projects. If your descriptive copy didn't grab your audience, consider turning over your ideas to a professional marketing copywriter for your next project. These people may cost you some money up front, but if they can make your next crowdfunding campaign more successful it will have been money well spent. Simply add their costs into what you set as your goal for the next campaign.

There is great value in running a crowdfunding campaign even if it doesn't achieve full funding. You put forth the effort to let people know about your talents. You learned some things about your own strengths and weaknesses. You completed a complex campaign and focused on marketing instead of just creating. You overcame some personal insecurities and fears.

Most of all, you learned about one of the most powerful sources of funding creative projects that exists. The next campaign will be much easier to develop and will be stronger because of what you learned from running the first campaign.

Regardless of how financially successful your first crowdfunding campaign was, make it just the *first!* Don't stop believing in yourself and what you have to bring to the world. If your art has merit you *will* find an audience for it.

Just as you continually learn how to become better at your creative endeavors use a crowdfunding campaign to better your marketing skills. After all, who would know the name Michelangelo if he hadn't been able to convince his patrons to back his projects?

As an artist, strive to bring something of value to the world. Make a difference through your creativity. We are all enriched when creative people share their talents, so don't be afraid to share yours. Remember, it is not the most talented, it is the best marketers who succeed.

"Dreams are of little value unless they are pursued."

- Tom Schneider

7 The Cash for Creatives System All Summed Up

In the preceding pages you've learned several ways to find the money you need to bring your creative dreams to life. We've taken you step by step through everything you'll need to create a successful crowdfunding project. Now it is just a matter of getting started. This is the moment in time when you can set yourself up for success!

Begin by putting an end to sabotaging your creative endeavors. Don't let careless everyday spending bleed you of your financial resources.

Discover **Found Money** through wise spending to help you function more economically every day and ease your financial stress.

Plan and advertise classes and workshops to generate **Fast Money** for when you need the extra cash. These classes can often turn into even more lucrative consulting jobs or consignment projects.

Set up your own personal crowdfunding site for the **Free Money** you need to fund the project you are passionate about. If you want assistance with your project, hire a coach or other professional to help you present your creative work in the best light possible to give your project the greatest chance of being funded. The coaching fees can be added into the amount you plan to raise. This could be your career launcher!

Once you have your project funded, DO IT! Follow through quickly and be gracious to your backers. They are your newly formed list of patrons. If they liked your work well enough to back it and you give them quality rewards they are apt to want to purchase other things that you create.

Nurture a relationship with these backers. At least once a month send them an update on your career. Send them notices when you are doing a show, when you are teaching a class or when you are featured in a magazine or gallery. They now have a vested interest in your career. They believe in you!

Finally, let us know about your project. We love to see what other people are doing to pursue their creative goals. While we always pledge $100 to support our coaching clients, we occasionally support other projects as well that we find especially compelling.

It is always gratifying when one of our coaching clients - or someone who reads this book - lets us know about their project and their successes using the techniques we have shown them. Our goal in writing this book is to encourage you to follow your creative dreams and bring them to reality. Let us know about them. We just might help you along the way.

"Positive thinking will get you started but often it takes coaching, followed by action, to get you to your goal."

- Lindy Schneider

8 Crowdfunding Coaching Program

Tom and I occasionally (as time permits) accept a small number of clients into our *Cash for Creatives Coaching Program,* by invitation only. If you are interested in having us consider you as one of our coaching clients we request you complete an application telling us about yourself and your project.

Send us an email at:

application@cashforcreatives.com

and we'll send you an application form. Once completed, send it back to us. It will be reviewed by our staff and you will be contacted regarding whether we can take you on as a client.

We are very selective about our coaching clients and have a very limited amount of clients due to our personal time constraints. We want to make sure we can dedicate our full efforts to those projects we choose to take on.

Please understand that we may have to turn down some very worthy projects. This does not mean your idea isn't valuable or that we don't think you can fund your dreams. It simply means we can't help everyone who asks.

Regardless of whether or not we decide to take on your project in our coaching program, we *will* contact you and let you know our decision. We know how important these dreams are (we've had them ourselves) and promise to let you know whether you are accepted into our *Cash for Creatives Coaching Program* or not.

Due to the number of applications we may receive we aren't able to give reasons for any declined projects or offer critiques on projects we don't accept. You may have a great idea and we simply don't have the time to take it on!

If you would just like to make us aware of a creative project you are putting up on a crowdfunding site you can also reach us at:

www.CashForCreatives.com

Go to the *Contact Us* tab and let us know about your crowdfunding campaign. If we find it compelling we may back your project even if you are not a client of our *Cash for Creatives Coaching Program.* We had several people we didn't know back our *Starfish on the Beach* campaign simply because they wanted to support the project and the positive message it brings.

We hope we have inspired and encouraged you to pursue your creative passion. You have the tools in this book to bring your creative dreams to life. Now it's time for you to take that bold step and get started. We look forward to the opportunity of seeing *your* dream project on one of the crowdfunding sites soon!

About the Authors:

Lindy is a best-selling author and award winning illustrator. Her work has appeared in magazines and books for clients such as Chicago Magazine, Ford Times, Zondervan Music and Worth Publishers. Lindy is also a contributing author for several of the New York Times #1 Best Selling *Chicken Soup for the Soul* series books and an award winning playwright.

Tom L. Schneider is an Amazon best-selling author and speaker. Tom has worked as both a technical and feature writer for numerous companies and publications. He has also won national awards for marketing and sales.

As co-founders of the *Cash for Creatives System,* Tom and Lindy provide coaching, strategy and motivation for artists, actors, and other creatives to achieve their potential. If you are interested in having Tom and Lindy coach you with your creative project, email us at Application@CashForCreatives.com and request an application.

We'll send you all the details about what is included in the coaching program.

Other Books by Tom and Lindy Schneider:

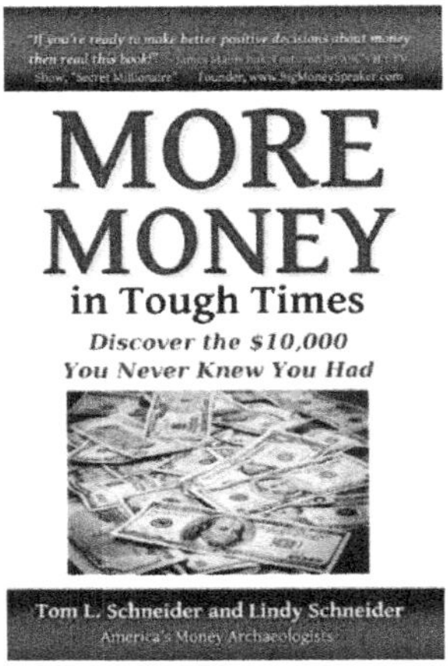

MORE MONEY in Tough Times: Discover the $10,000 You Never Knew You Had
(Part of the MORE MONEY Series by Peaks Publishing)

Learn how making simple changes to your spending can help you find more money in your pocket at the end of the year.

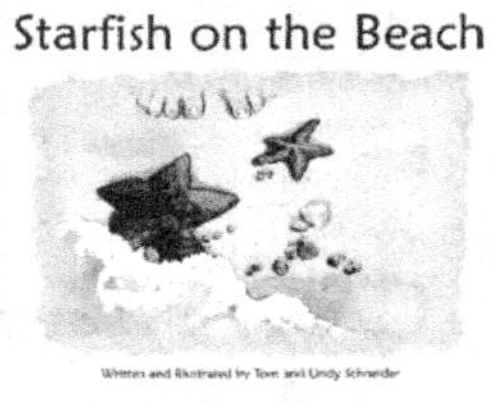

Starfish on the Beach
An Amazon Best Selling children's book

This inspirational book is a retelling of a familiar story of how everyone can make a difference.

All books by Lindy and Tom L. Schneider are available on Amazon.com and at the publisher's website:

www.PeaksPublishing.com

Contact Tom and Lindy at the following website:

www.CashForCreatives.com

Click on the Contact Us tab and send us an email. You can also post comments on our site.

To book Tom and Lindy to speak at your next event:

Both Tom L. and Lindy Schneider are accomplished speakers and trainers. They are available to speak for colleges, business groups, churches, associations, non-profits and schools.

For more information about our speaking schedule or to book a training or presentation, contact Tom and Lindy at the website above.

Notes

Notes

Notes

Made in the USA
Monee, IL
04 November 2026

67385548R00095